Email: contact@2doubleccies.com

Your CCIE Lab Success Strategy

The Non-Technical Guide Book

By

Dean Bahizad
CCIE 18887 (R&S, SP)

Vivek Tiwari
CCIE 18616 (R&S, SP)

contact@2doubleccies.com

Copyright

Warranty and Disclaimer

Trademark Acknowledgments

Praise for "Your CCIE Lab Success Strategy"

Kenya Thomas , CCSI #34027

"A behind the scenes guide on how to obtain your Cisco CCIE from two double CCIE's. No bull. No hype. Just the absolute truth about what it takes to become a CCIE. An absolute must have for anyone serious about pursuing their CCIE certification. Unlike anything else in the market! (Their preparation timelines alone are worth the price of the book). Get it now!"

Benjamin T. Parrish, CCIE# 11435

"There are business resources and practices that make the act of preparing for the CCIE easier, or even possible. The thought process that this book outlines, assists with those aspects which we, as technical folks, often don't consider."

Glenn Sharpnack, CCIE Candidate

"This amazingly easy to read book provides the non-technical insight needed to pass the CCIE lab exam. I recommend anyone pursuing a CCIE to read it before beginning lab exam preparation and closely follow the do's, don'ts, and the timeline."

Tahir Awan, CCIE#12680

"The book flows perfectly. A great behind the scenes look at the CCIE experience! Dean and Vivek have put forth the CCIE mind-set in an eloquent way. A master piece."

Sun-Ly Du, *CCIE Candidate*

"This book leads you straight to the point, and the powerful strategies make the difference between a pass or fail in the CCIE lab. This book really gave me a clear timeline to prepare for my CCIE."

What other reviewers have said:

- ✓ *The advice that is found in this book is not found in any CCIE book!*

- ✓ *After reading this book I feel that CCIE is within my reach.*

- ✓ *This unique book covers the much needed non-technical aspects of CCIE lab exam preparation.*

- ✓ *This type of mentorship from two CCIEs is priceless.*

- ✓ *This book lets me know when I am ready for the Lab exam.*

- ✓ *I will most certainly use this book for my second CCIE!*

About The Authors

Vivek Tiwari CCIE # 18616
(Routing and Switching and Service Provider)

Vivek Tiwari holds a Bachelor's degree in Physics, MBA and many certifications from multiple vendors including Cisco's CCIE. With double CCIE on R&S and SP track under his belt he mentors and coaches other engineers. Vivek has been working in Inter-networking industry for more than fifteen years, consulting for many Fortune 100 organizations. These include service providers, as well as multinational conglomerate corporations. His five plus years of service with Cisco's Advanced Services has gained him, the respect and admiration of colleagues and customers alike. His experience includes and not limited to network architecture, training, operations, management and customer relations; which made him a sought after coach & mentor, as well as a recognized leader. Vivek is currently engaged in consulting work for public sector.

Bayan Dean Bahizad CCIE # 18887
(Routing and Switching and Service Provider)

Dean Bahizad has a Bachelor of Applied Science (Engineering Honors) degree, and has been working with networks for more than fifteen years. His experience includes working on complex global networks as a Network Consulting Engineer for many fortune 100 companies. Dean has worked on financial institutions, automotive, manufacturing, and Service Provider segment. Dean has been with Cisco for the five plus years as a Consulting Engineer and Educational Specialist for both segments 1 Accounts and Service Providers. As an Educational Specialist, Dean has travelled around the globe in five continents and has worked closely with many Tier 1 Service Providers on training and deploying high-end equipment, such as CRS1/CRS3, CRS Multi-Chassis and ASR platform. Dean's talent is evident in his customer engagement, as the ability to deliver complex technologies in a simple, clear, and precise manner. If you have been in one of his classes you will know why people say you can laugh and learn at the same time.

contact@2doubleccies.com

Acknowledgements

We would like to thank Donna Menna, our editor for converting our engineer-speak into an understandable and printable language.

We would also like to give a special thank you to Neeka Karimian, Daria Karimian and Avantika Tiwari for their help with the final editing.

We thankfully acknowledge the helpful review and suggestions from:

Kenya Thomas

Tahir Awan

Sun-Ly Du

Glenn Sharpnack

Charlie Ball

Benjamin Parrish

We also want to extend our gratitude to Daria, Bahi, Neeka, Nadia, Mateen and Ben Karimian for their hospitality and endless supply of tea, coffee, food and friendship for all those long days and nights we were working on this book.

Lastly, we would like to thank everyone else who assisted and encouraged us with this work.

contact@2doubleccies.com

Dedication:

Vivek Tiwari: I would like to dedicate this book to my parents and my in-laws. Your inspiration, teachings and blessings have been the invisible hand guiding me forward all my life.

Dean Bahizad: I would like to dedicate this to my entire family who has supported me through all of the ups and downs of life. You offer great encouragement and I would not be where I am without all of the blessings that the Almighty has bestowed upon my family and me. A special thanks to my best friend and soulmate who has been there throughout this entire journey. To Anisa and Ariana who bring joy and love into my life each and every day.

contact@2doubleccies.com

Table of Contents

INTRODUCTION

A Wiseman once said, "Regard man as a mine rich in gems of inestimable value. Education can, alone, cause it to reveal its treasures, and enable mankind to benefit therefrom." This book was written in order for you to become empowered and to understand what lays ahead in your CCIE journey.

To start off let us explain what is CCIE? The Cisco Certified Internetworking Expert (CCIE) is an elite certification and is recognized worldwide as the top certification in networking. Some say this is the doctoral of networking and for many of us who have attempted or have gone through this journey can testify to this fact. This certification not only proves your technical prowess but also adds prestige to your résumé. It may increase your salary, and provide job security in today's environment. It has been stated that over the past ten years, more than half of the engineers who passed the written exam did not pass the lab exam; and for the ones who attempted the lab it took at least three attempts to pass the CCIE lab.

After we completed two different CCIE lab certification tracks, we realized an important element (the non-technical aspects) was missing in all of the training material. This element has not been taught anywhere; until now. We have created this unique book to discuss the non-technical aspects of the CCIE lab. This book is for anyone, who is either considering taking on the CCIE challenge, or has passed the written portion of the exam. It is for those who have failed the lab and it is for those who already have a CCIE and are considering pursuing another CCIE track.

We want to tell you at the outset that we are engineers just like you, and because of that, this book is short and to the point. In our experience, we have seen CCIE candidates approach the lab exam just like any other exam. Due to the enormity of this exam, some get sidetracked or discouraged. In many instances, this is due to the non-technical aspects. Here are a few common scenarios that we have seen.

Scenario 1:

You plan and set a target date for scheduling your CCIE lab and start studying very hard. As you approach your target date, you realize that you are not fully prepared and so you postpone scheduling the CCIE lab. After doing this a couple of times you stop trying.

The problem in this scenario is that your target date is not planned well. Either the date is too aggressive or you are not able to devote as much time for studying. Both of these are non-technical reasons that we will tackle in this book.

Scenario 2:

You start preparing after reading the Lab blueprint. The sheer number of books you have to read tells you that this is difficult. After reading three or four books you realize that you have already started to forget things from the first book. When this happens, you may get overwhelmed and stop studying altogether.

The problem in this scenario is that you need to change the way you prepare and study for the CCIE Lab. You need to be very specific about what training resources to use, and how to use them. This is another non-technical aspect. We will give you guidelines on how to maximize your studying efficiency later on in this book.

Scenario 3:

For your specific CCIE track you may purchase training lab books which may have 20, 30 or even 40 labs to choose from. You setup the lab using simulators; for example DYNAMIPS or GNS3 to practice with. You soon realize that although you know the answers, you still do not understand why a particular task was completed in a specific manner. As you complete more and more of these labs you recognize there are many gaps in your knowledge and you have to start fresh by reading up on technologies. This may cause you to postpone or give up on your CCIE quest.

The problem in this scenario is that the candidate has many gaps in his or her knowledge. By jumping into the labs without proper planning and preparation, the labs become more daunting. This book addresses the gradual step-by-step processes you should follow in order to succeed and understand the lab.

Scenario 4:

You are a great engineer and are on top of your game. Because of this, you are always busy and have many responsibilities. This leaves you with very little time for studying. You can spare two or three weeks max so you decide to take a one week CCIE boot camp from a leading training provider and schedule your lab two weeks after that. After completing the course, you realize that you need much more time to study, a luxury you don't find yourself having.

In this scenario, scheduling and planning study time while having a full time job is the roadblock, and we tell you how to get around that, and share our own stories.

We can keep on going with many more scenarios; these and many other pitfalls are addressed in this book.

This guidebook gives you the strategies that have been successfully used by us for both our CCIEs, along with real life examples. We tell you:

- The three essential keys to unlock your success.

- How to effectively utilize your training provider's resources.

- The four step process that will help when using Video on Demand.

- The necessary preparation to start your hands-on labs.

- How to speed up learning using a partner.

- The Do's and Don'ts for your CCIE lab preparation.

- Five sample timelines for preparing for your CCIE.

- How you can do all of this, and work full time.

This book is easy to follow. What we have written is advice that we gave to others about our CCIE experience. It contains short concise chapters that will not take away your study time.

All of the chapters in this book are suggestions based on our successful personal experiences. Use these suggestions to suit your specific needs. Remember these are suggestions, and not hard set rules to help you succeed in your CCIE lab.

If you have a huge task which is outside of your comfort zone, you need to break it down into smaller manageable chunks. At times, you may feel overwhelmed, but you need to be in control and rationalize the purpose behind this undertaking. This reminds me [(Dean)] of a story that my Italian father in-law told me on our occasional long walks. He lived in the mountainous region of Roccamorice, Italy, and had to climb the mountain for his daily chores. His little legs ached and he complained to his grandmother and asked her to carry him up the mountain. His grandmother lovingly encouraged him to not look at how much further he had to go, but to just keep climbing. Put your head down, watch where you are going and before you know it, you are at the summit. Once you follow our guidelines and decide on what path to take, your sole job is to be persistent and aggressively pursue a plan, without looking at the distance that you have traveled or the long road ahead.

We recognize that CCIE is usually a twelve month project that you need to break down into daily activities and goals. Thus the question that you should be asking yourself is, "What can I do in the next fifteen minutes to help with my daily goal?" This question changes the way you look at things, namely chopping down CCIE into fifteen minute intervals. The goal is to get a CCIE but what you need to realize is that every fifteen minutes counts and can bring you one step closer.

This guidebook will give you an inside view of CCIE Lab preparation. We will be mentoring you through a step by step process and provide answers to the questions you will have on your journey to this demanding certification. Some ideas in this book may sound deceivingly simple, yet they will make a huge difference once you implement them rather than just attempting the lab exam. For example, it is important before heading to bed, you spend five to ten minutes of your time reflecting on what you did for that day and write down your plan for the next day. This simple gesture will prepare you for the next day and get you started on the right foot.

We are here to give you the straightforward, no-nonsense picture of what it will take to get your CCIE. These strategies have worked for us twice, and we are confident that they will help you in your endeavor too.

Visit our website at **2doubleccies.com** for additional information.

CHAPTER 1: DO YOU REALLY WANT TO BE A CCIE?

Since you are reading this, you are obviously considering the CCIE lab exam. In writing this book, we wanted to inform you on what to expect in the simplest terms. No sugarcoating. No exaggeration. Just a **frank conversation from one engineer to another**.

When talking to other engineers about CCIE—whether it is those who have obtained it, those who have failed to obtain it, or even those who have just considered obtaining it—you invariably hear some or all of the following comments:

1. It is a lot of work.

2. CCIE certification is not worth the time and money it takes to earn it. (Not true)

3. When studying for the CCIE exam, 24 hours a day doesn't seem like nearly enough time.

4. You must focus on CCIE and nothing else.

5. You must be rich to take the CCIE exam because it is ridiculously expensive.

6. The CCIE exam is very difficult and designed for you to fail.

7. Only a small percentage of candidates even pass the CCIE lab exam.

8. I failed my exam because of a bug in the IOS.

9. I failed my exam because the hardware was faulty.

10. I failed my exam because the test evaluation is flawed.

Are all of these comments true? Of course not; some of the above statements are made by individuals to justify why they are not CCIE's. Obtaining a CCIE number is definitely a formidable task, requiring untold hours of study and sacrifice over an extended period of time (usually eight to twelve months). In spite of that, do you still want to be a CCIE? If your answer is "yes", why? Ask yourself that, then list at least the top five reasons in the space we have provided on the next page. If you can think of more, list them as well. Take out a piece of paper, if you need to. This list will help you isolate your reasons, and even solidify them in your own mind. More importantly, it will give you something to refer to in the future, especially if you do seriously decide to go for your CCIE number. Because there will be times where you feel discouraged, or lose focus, or wonder why you are working so hard. In those instances, you can return to this **list to remind yourself** of the benefits.

Your Top-Five Reasons for Becoming a CCIE

1. _____

2. _____

3. _____

4. _____

5. _____

Those who have become CCIEs agree that the exam takes a lot of work and a serious commitment, but they also agree that the results are worth it. When talking to them, they may describe some of the difficulties they encountered, but they will also explain how they were able to work around them. They are proud of their achievement, and if you were to ask them "what are the most important qualities a successful candidate must possess?" they will almost invariably say a positive attitude and an unwavering commitment.

CHAPTER 2: A TALE OF TWO ENGINEERS

Before we delve any deeper into this book, I [(Vivek)] want to tell you a true story about two engineers I know. To protect their identities, I have changed a few personal references and altered events slightly.

Charlie (Engineer 1) is a young guy in his 30s in the desktop support group. I met him only because I broke my laptop keyboard and he came to my desk with a replacement. While repairing it, he asked me about my role in the company. I told him about LAN and WAN technologies, routers, and switches. I thought this would be a short, five-minute conversation, but he was very curious, and it went on for over half an hour. He listened to me as intently as he could while dismantling my laptop and replacing the broken keyboard. He was intelligent, curious, and inquisitive. I pointed him towards CCNA, and even scrounged up an old book on the subject that I had lying around.

He went home and read the book, and came back asking questions. I answered him as well as I could, but his thirst for knowledge was unquenchable. He went on to buy other books, and began peppering the other engineers in my group with questions. He became a CCNA in about four months—a real CCNA, not the kind who simply absorbs brain dumps in order to pass the exam.

As he progressed toward his CCNP, he was most interested to find out what issues and challenges we had faced in our own CCIE-level labs. We let him loose in our lab in the evenings, and, to our surprise, he would often stay overnight working on whatever problems we had posed to him.

I moved on from the company, but met Charlie again about two years later. Was he a CCIE? I'll let you guess.

Andy (Engineer 2) was also a young guy in his 30s, and an experienced engineer. He impressed all of us during his job interview, and joined our team. He had a great attitude towards learning, and possessed a great depth of knowledge. He was also never afraid to ask questions.

When he joined our team, he was working toward his CCNP, but he was certainly CCIE material. He achieved his CCNP within months, and our boss was so impressed with his performance and dedication, that he asked him to try for his CCIE. He started studying for it immediately. Two weeks before his scheduled CCIE written exam date, he was given paid time off to prepare for it. He worked hard, and passed it easily.

Satisfied by his success, we encouraged him to attend a CCIE lab boot camp, which he did. When he was finished, he leapt right into the CCIE practice labs. He believed he was doing so well with them, that he decided to take the actual CCIE lab exam the following month. He worked really hard, sticking around every day after office hours to study and practice his labs. Even on his days off, he VPN'd into the lab.

As the date of his lab exam approached, he requested two weeks off in order to prepare for it. He failed, and felt discouraged. He confided in me that the exam opened his eyes and made him realize just how much harder he had to work for it, how much more he had to study. We all assured him that failing a first attempt at the exam is not at all unusual, that, in fact, it usually takes two or three attempts. We encouraged him to continue his study, and even offered any guidance or assistance that he needed, but the failure had taken its toll on his confidence. He continued to study, but, more and more often, other obligations—familial, financial, and occupational— began to compete for his time, and even take precedence.

Looking at these two examples, which engineer do you think has become a CCIE?

Hint: Charlie does not need to and will not read this book unless I ask him to.

As you may have guessed, Charlie went on to pass his exam, while Andy, a year and a half later, has not. Andy, in other words, will in all likelihood read this book because it will help him overcome some of the obstacles to getting his CCIE.

Charlie got his CCIE within three years, which was a remarkable feat, and a big blow to my ego because I had more experience and it had taken me much longer. After learning of his success, I sought out some of my old colleagues and inquired about Charlie. What I heard was an astonishing story of dedication, perseverance, and continuous improvement. It was like something out of a book or a movie. Charlie had spent so much time studying, he had learned as much in three years as I had in seven or eight. One of the biggest factors to his success, besides a nearly all-consuming commitment, was an ideal environment. He had unfettered access to lab equipment and actual CCIE engineers who were eager to assist him and answer his questions anytime he asked.

Andy, on the other hand, also had access to equipment and engineers, but he let other factors get in the way. Some of these factors were external—obligations to family, friends, and work—but some of them were internal. Failing his first lab exam had taken a serious toll on his confidence. Perhaps his goal had even begun to seem unattainable. He continued to study, but not as often. Something else always seemed to come up. In the meantime, he suffered another major setback—the blue-print of the lab exam changed. He had to buy a whole new set of updated training materials, and learn an entirely new set of topics. End result: he is still not a CCIE!

Both of these engineers were intelligent and decided that they wanted to become CCIEs. Andy even had the benefit of a company-sponsored boot camp and paid time-off to study. But Charlie had **perseverance and an unwavering commitment**. He had not let anything get in his way, not even failure.

Perhaps you are thinking that Andy will be able to identify himself by our description. Unfortunately, this could not be farther from the truth. Stories like his are all too common. We have seen it, and many variations of it, many times over the years. That is why we wanted to write this book. We wanted to help you avoid some of these common obstacles to achieving your CCIE. This book is the distillation of many years of experience, ours and our colleagues—men and women with many different skill sets, study habits, and from many different countries—and we hope that you will learn as much from it as you will from any technical book that you may have purchased.

CHAPTER 3: WHY THIS BOOK

When we began our quest for the coveted CCIE number, we heard many of the statements in "Chapter 1: Do You REALLY Want To Be a CCIE?" Some of them were from engineers who actually achieved their CCIE, but many of them were from those who had either failed the test, or never attempted to take it in the first place.

We were working for Cisco at the time and had access to a lot of CCIEs, both in our local team and extended teams. We also had the opportunity to work with other CCIEs on projects, architectural designs and troubleshooting issues. We even interviewed some CCIEs who'd taken the exam in the original, two-day format. They were very proud of their four-digit CCIE number. Some of the engineers we met had three, four, sometimes even five CCIE certification's, and some of them were the authors of their own books, and had multiple CCIE certification's for many years.

Being surrounded by these accomplished individuals left us inspired and motivated. We wanted to be a part of this elite group of men and women who hailed from five continents and scores of countries. We peppered them with questions, trying to learn their strategies for success. This book represents that cumulative experience and information.

It took Dean and I [(Vivek)] about eleven months to obtain our first CCIE, and seven months to obtain our second. We challenged each other and competed to see who would get to the goal first. I got my first CCIE before Dean, but he beat me to the second. We are both very competitive individuals, so challenging each other in this way worked well for us.

The problem is that CCIE engineers are highly intelligent, focused individuals who tend to fixate only on the technical aspects of certification. In our experience, we noticed that the non-technical side of the CCIE lab exam is just as important as the technical side. Whenever we are asked about our CCIE experience, we talk about the technical and the non-technical aspects, and, almost invariably, the non-technical aspects are valued more. While studying for our own CCIEs as well as talking to, tutoring, and inspiring many other candidates in their quest for certification, we realized that there were very few, if any, resources for this information. **This is the only book available that fills that non-technical gap.**

However, we also realize that each individual has a different approach to learning. We are simply writing about what worked for us and what resonated most with our fellow engineers. We encourage you to adapt this text to best suit your needs and style of learning. **Consider this more of a**

guidebook than an infallible set of rules to follow. For instance, from our experience and interviews with a number of other certified engineers, we suggest that after the basic background work, you should be able to attain your CCIE in less than a year (See: Chapter 37: Suggested Timelines for CCIE Preparation). This timeline is only a rough estimate. We have seen some engineers pass their CCIE lab exam in as little as three months, and others pass it in eighteen to twenty-four months. We also understand that, as of writing this book, the eight-hour CCIE Lab format is different for R&S as compared to Voice or Security. Nonetheless, the strategies in this book are still applicable and you can easily adjust them according to your needs.

CHAPTER 4: CCIE IS DIFFICULT BUT NOT IMPOSSIBLE

How difficult is it?

This is the question I [(Vivek)] am asked most often. My answer is always the same: It is difficult, definitely challenging, but certainly not impossible.

I have been in the internetworking industry since the days of ARCNET, which was before Ethernet—in short, for a very long time. I've met many top-notch engineers who were able to get their CCIEs. I've also met many other engineers, equally brilliant, who could not get a CCIE, despite their obvious intelligence, experience, and talent. From my interactions with many of them, I knew that they had a command of whatever technology they dealt with and great work experience. I just couldn't figure out how they failed the exam. This told me that the CCIE lab couldn't just be about knowing the technologies involved, there must be something more.

I thought that, perhaps, those who failed simply knew too much and interpreted the questions in an entirely different way than the test intended. I can say from personal experience that the way you think, plan, and implement strategies under pressure has a direct influence on your results. But sometimes you need to think outside of the box in order to solve any given task.

The problem is, **many engineers restrict their mindset to real-world solutions**. For example, they would never consider trying a different encoding on a serial link or redistributing BGP into their IGP, because that just isn't done on real networks. This isn't a real production network, it's a lab. **You've got to put best practices aside**. You don't have to concern yourself with scalability of the network or stress-test with traffic. Remember, it does not have to work in the real world; it just has to work in the lab, nothing more, and nothing less.

All of the CCIEs we've met are just good engineers, like you and me. They too make mistakes and learn from them. What makes them different is that they took up this challenge, worked hard for it, and maintained a laser-like focus on it until they reached their goal. That CCIE number is now theirs for life. **No one can take it away** from them.

What We Did (by Vivek)

We understood early on that there is no shortcut to get a CCIE number. Indeed, all of the CCIEs we talked to told us we would have to work very hard, so every time we suffered a setback or a failure (and we had many), we realized that they were just a part of the process and redoubled our efforts.

I remember one time Dean was working on one of the full, eight-hour practice labs and got stuck about five hours into it. He spent about an hour troubleshooting, but just could not make it work. He grew frustrated, then called me, as usual. I listened to his tale, and then called him an irritating—and unrepeatable—name, which upset him. He got quiet.

"Uh-oh!" I thought, "I pushed him too hard." So I told him not to give up, and that I would help him.

He informed me, firmly and indignantly, that he was *not* giving up, and then hung up.

He called me again about four in the morning, saying that he had completed the practice lab, and that he did not ever want to hear me call him that name again.

I asked him what the problem had been and he said he didn't know. Puzzled, I said, "If you don't know what the problem was, how did you solve it?"

Dean laughed and said that he'd just started all over again from scratch, and that it went smoothly the second time. Apparently, he'd rested for two hours, then worked through the night to complete the lab. Had I not called him that unrepeatable name, he would have given up.

I suppose it could be said that he did not actually solve his original problem, but he didn't need to. He'd been able to conquer his idea of giving up, and proved to himself that he could succeed. Those eighteen hours made a huge difference. They gave him the boost of confidence needed to continue working toward his CCIE.

For the record, Dean had gotten into the habit of saving all of those non-working lab configurations, and was later able to isolate the particular issue that had plagued him during this lab.

The CCIE is an all-or-nothing proposition. You either give it total commitment, and pass, or you don't, and fail.

CHAPTER 5: INVESTING IN CCIE CERTIFICATION

Pay the Piper But Don't Mortgage the House

There is a saying: you have to make a large investment to get a great return. Getting your CCIE may seem expensive, but if you compare it to getting a bachelor's degree at a U.S. school, you'll see that it's actually not as expensive. Indeed, the return on investment for your CCIE may be substantially greater.

Think about it. Depending on the university or college you choose, you could be looking at spending anywhere between $20,000 and $60,000 and four years of your life to obtain a bachelor's degree. On the other hand, getting your CCIE may cost you between $5,000 and $10,000 and only one year of your life, depending on how many times you have to take the test, and how many distractions you can avoid.

It should be noted, though, that we are not advocating getting your certification instead of a bachelor's degree. On the contrary, in this day and age, a bachelor's degree is essential. We're simply comparing the costs and the relative value added. Having a bachelor's degree *and* a CCIE is an ideal combination, and in great demand.

The CCIE, however, does offer many great advantages, and not all of them are financial. It will enable you to command a larger salary, and certainly allow you to move up in your career path; but it will also bring you much recognition from your peers.

People always ask us if the CCIE was worth our investment, and we always say "yes", without hesitation.

Now, even though getting your CCIE may be much cheaper than getting your bachelor's degree, there *are* substantial costs associated with it and it's very important to plan your approach and create a budget.

Below is a short list of expenses you should keep in mind while making your decision on whether or not to pursue your CCIE or when estimating the costs of it.

1. CCIE lab training resources, such as Video on Demand and/or Audio on Demand

2. Instructor-led classes or boot camps

3. CCIE lab examination fees

4. Air travel and hotel expenses for attempting the lab

5. CCIE related reference books

6. CCIE lab simulation hardware and software

7. Rack rental or equipment costs

This list is by no means comprehensive. Consider it a rough guide to the overall expenses you can expect. Feel free to add or subtract items according to your situation and expectations. The good news is that the CCIE is one certification many companies are willing to pay for, at least in part.

When planning financially for your CCIE lab, **plan for at least two or three attempts.** I'm not saying this to discourage you, but because failure on the first or second attempt is all-too-common, and I ^(Dean) don't want you to have to abandon all of your hard work and sacrifices due to financial issues.

You should also make it your mission to **find out your company's policy concerning their employee's continuing education and elite certification programs**. Many companies (Cisco, its partners particularly and Service Providers) offer financial assistance for CCIE lab attempts. In some cases, they may cover all of the costs, in others, only some of them. It's up to you to find out which, if any, your company provides. You may have to make a case to your company as to why they should invest their money into your enterprise. In these instances, you should outline all of the benefits the company will see with a certified engineer on staff. Be sure to have your manager advocate your case to his or her superiors.

Explore all avenues. Often, there are many hidden resources and policies within any organization that you may not even be aware of. **Check**

the continuing education budget to see if certification falls within that category or subcategory. Talk to your manager and your HR manager and find out what's available. Remember, the squeaky wheel gets the grease. Make your intentions known.

Many large service providers, and all Cisco Gold and Silver Partners, are required to have CCIEs on staff. This means that the demand for CCIEs is great, and so is the potential that one of them will sponsor your efforts.

A good friend told me years ago that you have to start looking at certification as a business and sell it as such. If you do it right, you may receive not just all of the lab expenses incurred, but also time off for studying, travel costs, and even company rewards and a recognition letter to you and your department executive.

Lastly, I'd like to insist that you do not mortgage your house in order to pay for your CCIE. This may sound like a no-brainer, but we actually know an engineer that did this.

CCIE is a very good investment, but just like any other investment, it has its pros and cons. Do not make this move unless you have absolutely no other options and the rewards are completely worth the risk to you. We have given you plenty of options in this chapter, and there are hundreds of other avenues available that you should seriously consider before you even entertain the idea of mortgaging your home. Do not make any final decision on it until you've exhausted all other possibilities.

What We Did (by Vivek)

For the record, Dean and I both worked for Cisco when we completed our CCIEs, and Cisco did provide an incentive for those of us who pursued certification. Despite that, both of us always set aside 7 to 10% of our salaries towards continuing education. Before we began the endeavor, we estimated all of our costs and were committed to moving forward, even if it meant we would have to make multiple attempts.

CHAPTER 6: WHAT HAPPENS WHEN YOU GET YOUR CCIE?

What Should I Expect?

Getting your CCIE means instant credibility. Suddenly, you become an expert in your group. You've learned so much from studying for the CCIE that there are usually few engineers around you who will have as much current knowledge. Your understanding of different technologies gives you a large arsenal of tools with which to design networks and troubleshoot problems in a faster and more reliable way. Now, people will not hesitate to bring their network problem to you, nor hesitate to solicit your advice or look to you for guidance. They won't have any reservations about granting you absolute access to their most secure networks.

In short, you will be instantly transformed from a trained doctor into a neurosurgeon. When you talk, others will listen.

With your new, hard-won status, you will realize that you have much more confidence when suggesting changes to current and future network designs. You will now be called upon to attend all those design meetings, and will be expected to play a pivotal role. You will also see a spike in productivity.

If you are in pre-sales or sales, you will notice that your opinion carries more weight. You will be selling more, and you will be busier than ever, as more and more customers seek out your opinion.

All of this really means that you **will have much greater job satisfaction**, and overall confidence.

Many companies, such as Cisco and Cisco Partners, offer attractive rewards for those who obtain a CCIE, which means more money. CCIEs in the U.S. can easily earn in the range of $100,000 to $140,000 annually, depending on their experience, city of residence, and, of course, the organization for which they work.

Your business cards will carry the CCIE logo, as well as your CCIE number, and you can expect your colleagues to invite you to lunch or to dinner in order to solicit your professional opinion. Pre-sales engineers, account managers, and even Directors of Sales may seek your input and recommendations as well. Your name will appear in presentations that the sales force uses to sell partner services.

In short, if you work **for a Cisco partner, you will be their crowning jewel**. You will become well known in your organization, and each and every task you accomplish after that will only add to your fame.

Finally, you will no longer have to worry about job security. During tough economic times, when corporations start cutting back their workforce, CCIEs are usually the last to go. That is because **organizations try their hardest to hold onto their most talented technical people**. On the off-chance that you are laid off, you will most likely be rehired immediately by a competitor. Evidence for this can be seen in our most recent economic collapse. While the United States and the world in general went through its toughest economic condition since the Great Depression, with unemployment at near-record levels, there was still a strong demand for skilled CCIEs.

What We Did (by Dean)

As soon as Vivek and I [(Dean)] announced our CCIE success, we started receiving congratulatory emails from our colleagues. And as the news spread farther afield, we got them from old friends, and the engineers and managers and our customers. Our company rewarded us with plaques and other incentives like the CCIE jacket.

We started getting job offers, both from within our own companies, and from others. With a renewed sense of confidence, we engaged in our work, and found doors opening up for us that we had never even thought of, which allowed us to move ahead in our careers quicker than ever.

After taking some time off to spend with our families, Vivek pursued a career in Cisco Advanced Services as an automotive lead for a Tier One account, while I accepted an opportunity to travel around the world as an Educational Specialist at Cisco Advanced Services where I worked with many different organizations and Tier One service providers.

CHAPTER 7: THE CIRCLE OF TRUST

Engaging Everyone In Your Inner Circle

Before you take the plunge and pursue your CCIE, you should make absolutely certain that everyone in your life supports your decision, especially your spouse, your children and your closest friends and family members. The CCIE requires total commitment, and without everyone's cooperation, it can be downright impossible to achieve. If you don't have their total support, perhaps you should consider delaying certification until circumstances are more amenable.

In that light, **you should consider certification a communal goal, rather than just a personal one.**

Consider this: On the very same day that one of our friends got his third CCIE, he also got his divorce papers.

This is an extreme example, but, unfortunately, all too true. If you are going to be able to work a full-time job, and still be able to study for four hours a night on weekdays, and ten or twelve hours on the weekends, then you are going to need everyone in your household to be behind you 100%, and 100% supportive.

Everyone in your life is going to have to make just as many sacrifices as you are. Together, you are all going to have to weigh these considerations before making a final decision. Remember, it isn't just about the time you won't be able to devote to family events. There is also a great physical and mental toll, as well as a financial one.

There will be times when you will need to rely on your family for emotional support, especially when you are feeling down or discouraged because you are not progressing as quickly as you thought. They must be your strength, and help you move forward.

Nothing in this chapter is meant to deter you from pursuing your CCIE. Rather, we just want you to be aware of everything you are going to encounter in the process. There are just as many benefits (aside from simply the financial ones you will encounter upon success) for your family as there are drawbacks. For instance, think about the positive example you will be setting for them, as well as for yourself. You will definitely learn and acquire a new sense of perseverance.

And if you make it a group goal, instead of a personal one, success will be something that everyone will be proud of.

What We Did (by Dean)

You must take into account that it will be your spouse/partner who will take up all of the slack while you're off studying, and that although they are not actually taking the exam themselves, the entire process will be just as stressful for them.

Within months of starting our first CCIE, Vivek and I ^(Dean) understood very early on the importance of getting everybody onboard. To compensate, we sat down with our families and told them of our plans and what to expect. We definitely did not want to be away from home for hours, only to return to great tension, and serious arguments. By having this open and honest discussion with our entire families, and laying out our plans and expectations, everyone understood that they all had an important role to play in our success.

While Dean was preparing for his first exam, his daughters were really young, and he felt like he was missing all of the major milestones. His wife, recognizing this, captured all of these missed moments in pictures and videos for him to share and enjoy.

The sacrifices that you make during this period will pay off when you pass the exam and find yourself with plenty of time to catch up. You will have your certification, and you and your family will have the satisfaction of having achieved it as a unit.

One thing we both found interesting, is that after we passed the exam, we found ourselves with so much free time on the weekends that we didn't know how to deal with it.

Both of us set a great example for our kids that you have to work hard for long periods of time to succeed.

CHAPTER 8: MANAGING EXTERNAL INFLUENCES

How To Deal With Road Blocks and Setbacks

Perhaps one of the biggest challenges to getting your CCIE is finding a way to mitigate all of the external forces that seek to blow you off course. You may experience a family emergency or an unexpected increase in your workload at the office, or sudden, unforeseen financial difficulties. These are just a few of the issues that could be waiting in the wings just to trip you up as you continue on your journey toward the coveted CCIE. Remember, studying for it can take a year or more. That's a lot of time for trouble to emerge.

To ensure that you stay on track (or as close to track as you can when circumstances suddenly change), **you should follow a timeline.** To help you do that, we've created five different timelines in Chapter 37 for you and included them at the end of this book. These timelines will not only give you a good estimate of how long a CCIE certification takes, but will also help you make sure that the time you spend studying is used most effectively and efficiently.

A timeline is basically a series of steps, and the estimated time it should take for you to complete them. If you don't stick as closely to these timelines as you can, things can go bad very quickly. For instance, most engineers start by reading the recommended books and learning the technologies related to their CCIE labs. So let's say you decided to read three of these big books over the next sixty days. You will automatically calculate that you'll need to read one book about every twenty days. If you procrastinate, that deadline will approach rapidly, and the pressure will begin to mount. If you don't finish that first book on time, chances are that you won't be able to finish the second book on time either and so on. Soon, it is day 40 and you haven't even finished that first book. The pressure now is almost unbearable. Any more delays and you may give up.

You mustn't let all of these pressures build up. The more anxious you feel, the less likely you will be to continue. Simply adjust your timeline for the current phase, but keep your CCIE lab date in place. If you are making too many adjustments, however, you must re-evaluate your approach. Try to figure out what is preventing you from adhering to the timeline. Perhaps you need to adjust your priorities, or just quit procrastinating.

As an example of how detrimental these delays can be to your success, we can take the example of one of Dean's students. This man spent his spring and summers coaching baseball. He was so committed to this, he told me, that he wasn't planning on studying for his CCIE at all during this time.

Six months out of every year were going to be set aside exclusively to focus on baseball. Naturally, what happened was, he'd take time off and, when he returned to his studies in the fall, he'd forgotten most of what he'd already learned. It was like starting all over again. Because his priorities clashed with his CCIE, he eventually gave up his dream of obtaining it.

Regardless of how much you plan and prepare, experiencing some kind of hiccup and setback is inevitable. Therefore, **it is important that you give priority to what really matters** and give yourself a little lead time. Please refer to Chapter 37 for the amount of lead time you can afford in the five different timelines we've provided. This is the amount of time that you can give to other priorities without throwing your timeline off (for a short duration only).

However, **you must not rely on that lead time** and use it as an excuse to slack or procrastinate. It is there only for emergencies, or those few issues that take precedence over your CCIE. If it can wait, or can be delegated, you should do so.

If you really want to achieve one of the toughest technical certifications in the world, **you've got to give it 100% period**. Movie nights, hanging out with your friends, or watching football should be a lower priority. If they are not, you should really reconsider pursuing your CCIE. Remember, you can always catch up with your friends and football scores, and anything else you might have missed, after you have your CCIE number.

For me [Dean], when my children were sick or needed to see the doctor, my wife and our support chain attended to them. I was not; however, too absorbed in my work to check up on them and make sure it wasn't anything serious. In any case, my family knew that I was just a phone call away.

One obstacle that might affect your focus is your chain of command, especially if they are less than supportive at times. Communicate with them on a regular basis and let them know of your progress in your job and your CCIE. **Let them advocate your interest in the organization.**

A former student of mine was studying for his second attempt at the lab exam. He had studied hard and believed he knew the material inside and out. As a consequence, he became very confident that he was going to pass and began celebrating prematurely. After the exam, the confidence continued. Although it was difficult, he still believed he'd done very well. A day later, he learned that he had failed. His boss was so surprised that he had failed; he told the student that, after two chances he would not support another attempt. This brought the situation to a crisis. The student had already suffered an emotional setback from failing, now he had the added burden.

A few harsh lessons can be found in this story. The first is, **don't allow yourself to become overconfident.** Remember that you can never know everything about all of the technologies. The second is to **keep your boss in the loop,** and set your expectations exceedingly low. Just because you are about to take the exam does not mean you are going to pass. You should also make sure that your boss and the entire company understands the benefits of having a CCIE as a team member. Remind them of the financial incentives to those Cisco partners that have CCIEs in their organizations.

What We Did (by Dean)

While working toward our second CCIE, Vivek got a call from my wife. She was worried about me because it was my birthday and she had tried repeatedly to reach me, but I was not answering my phone. I had left home early that day in order to finish some work so that I could make it to our study session on time. Amidst all of the chaos of trying to juggle all of these things, I forgot it was my birthday and accidentally left my phone in the car. I hadn't realized until that moment how utterly absorbed and focused we were in our quest for our second CCIE.

In another instance, we were at the office, working over a particularly vexing problem, when a snowstorm blew in. It was so intense that it closed all major highways within a half hour. Traffic was at a standstill. We watched all of this unfold from our office window, but continued studying, thinking that it'd just blow over, and crews would have the roads clear in a couple of hours. However, this did not happen.

Since things only seemed to be getting worse, we decided to pack up our stuff and head home. The snowstorm had been so bad that not even the road-clearing crews had been able to venture out into it. What's more, freezing rain had fallen on all of that unplowed snow creating a two-inch crust of ice over the top of it. It took me three crawling, careful hours to get home.

While my conscious mind was concerned with driving, my subconscious mind continued to work on our problem, until, a short while later; a solution suddenly came to me, seemingly from nowhere. Needless to say, I was excited and rather impatient to get home. I wanted to test my solution, but I already knew it would work.

As soon as I slammed the door, kicking the crust of snow off my shoes, I went straight to the phone, called Vivek, and revealed my solution. Within thirty minutes we had validated the solution.

CHAPTER 9: SET A CLEAR PRIZE FOR SUCCESS

Motorcycles, Cruises, and Vacations (Just Name It)

Since you are about to embark on one of the most challenging certifications of your life, you should establish some kind of material reward to help motivate you. Some examples could be:

1. Buying yourself a Harley-Davidson motorcycle

2. Add a swimming pool to your house

3. Taking your family on a cruise to the Santander, Palma De Mallorca (Spain), Jamaica, or Hawaii

4. Buying yourself a Rolex watch

You may be wondering why? After all, isn't the satisfaction you will feel upon passing the exam motivation enough? The answer is no. You see, the subconscious mind responds best to real, physical rewards—things that can be touched or felt. Also, it will only enhance your satisfaction. Every time you look at your new watch, ride your new Harley, or look at the family photos from the Santander cruise, you'll be reminded of your great accomplishment.

Whatever your reward, try to get a picture of yourself with it. Select a Harley and have the sales person take a picture of you sitting on it. Then inform him or her that you'll be back for it in about six months. The same goes for that Rolex watch. Go try it on, see how heavy it feels on your wrist. Get someone to take a picture. Of course, personal pictures aren't always possible, such as you on a cruise ship. In those cases, simply download a photo from the internet.

You should display these pictures prominently in your place of study, or anywhere else you will see them regularly. Tape them to the wall above your computer, or to the fridge, or the dashboard of your car. Carry one in your wallet. This will help give you a real, concrete goal.

What you are doing here is hanging a carrot in front of your face. **<u>Working for a real, tangible reward is often more effective than working toward some intangible certificate</u>**, and once you've selected your prize; one that you can see, feel, dream of or taste, your subconscious mind will automatically begin working toward it. What's more, when you finally reach your goal and get your reward, you will feel an even greater sense of accomplishment, one that will give you the confidence to go after your next great objective.

What We Did (by Dean)

Vivek wore a green Cisco band on his wrist for the duration of his CCIE study. He decided to remove it only when he got his CCIE number. The band eventually began to symbolize a shackle, one that prevented him from moving ahead in life. The only way he could break free was by reaching his goal.

Dean took his family out for extended road trip including a weekend to Niagara Falls, where the family booked the falls-view room of a premium hotel overlooking the falls and nightly fireworks. This trip gave the family the bonding that Dean felt they all needed.

CHAPTER 10: THE FIRST KEY

Set Your Goals and Write Them Down

In our experience, every network engineer wants to be a CCIE. Unfortunately, only a small number ever take and pass the written portion of the exam, and even fewer attempt the lab portion. They are all too often overwhelmed by many of the factors we've already warned you about. We don't want *you* to be overwhelmed, so here is what you do.

You are obviously going to set your goal at getting your CCIE number, but we want you to be more specific. We even want you to select a specific date. For instance, "I am going to get my CCIE number by December 19th, 2014." The more specific you are, the better it is.

As soon as you set this date, we want you to write it down. Post your goal (like the pictures of you and your tangible reward) where it will be easily visible to you. Make multiple copies if you have to, set it as the screensaver or background image on your computer.

You should then share your intentions with as many of your family, friends, and colleagues. What you are doing here is making your goals concrete, creating a public commitment, and holding yourself accountable.

The effectiveness of this strategy was recently established by a

Dominican University study.

You may have heard the story of a Harvard (or Yale) study that took place in the late 50s, 60s, or even 70s, in which the 3% of students who actually wrote down their goals were shown, 20 years later, to earn as much as ten times more than those who did not. This was discovered by Dominican University, and others, to be an urban legend, so they decided to test the hypothesis themselves. They took a group of 267 participants and broke them into five groups. Each of these groups was asked to adhere to a different level of commitment. The first group was asked to merely think about their goals. The second group was asked to think about their goal and write it down. The third group was asked to think about their goal, write it down, and establish action steps. The fourth group was asked to think about their goal, write it down, formulate action steps, and share their plan with a friend. The fifth group was asked to think about their goal, write it down, formulate action steps, share their plan with a friend, and then keep that friend updated on their progress as they pursued their goal.

In the end, the groups who simply put their goals on paper were significantly more likely to achieve their goals than those who did not, while those in group five were even more likely to succeed than any of the others.

If you'd like to read the study for yourself, you can see a summary here:

http://www.dominican.edu/dominicannews/study-backs-up-strategies-for-achieving-goals

I [(Vivek)] passed the CCIE written exam in 2000, and immediately began to prepare for the lab exam. I consulted many colleagues, friends, and anyone else I could find who had already attempted the lab. But what I didn't do was establish a firm date for taking it. Instead, I began buying books and hardware (since having your own was essential at the time). Because I was trying to save myself the financial burden of buying it all at once, it took me a long time to acquire it. By the time I was ready to set it up, the lab had changed. Some technologies, such as ISDN and Token Ring, were entirely removed from the lab blueprint. The CCIE lab workbook had changed.

All of this happened simply because I hadn't established a clear date for my goal. In the end, I essentially had to start all over, with different equipment and an entirely new training workbook.

For what it's worth, I still have many of those old 2500 routers in my basement.

It's human nature to procrastinate, to try to find the easy way out. We tend to postpone the most difficult tasks until an undetermined date in the future. To make matters worse, we live in an age in which everyone expects instant results. Nobody wants to wait for anything, especially not for months. The problem is, CCIE certification is a long-term commitment, and it's not going to get any easier as time passes. In fact, if anything CCIE is going to get harder as the new technology is introduced if you don't finish now, when will you?

The most important thing you can do is try to pass the exam before Cisco makes any major revisions to the test. Your CCIE lab training provider should be able to inform you of any expected changes. Be prepared.

What We Did

When we began our quest for our CCIE, we did not set a specific date because we didn't understand how important it was. However, we did learn a lot the first time around (the hard way, of course). When we were ready to start our second CCIE (Service Provider) quest, we immediately set ourselves to a specific date. By establishing a deadline for ourselves early on, we started preparing for the exam in the winter of 2008, and managed to reach our goal by the spring of 2009.

CHAPTER 11: THE SECOND KEY

Visualize; Behave As If You've Already Achieved It

I ^(Vivek) am a big believer in the power of visualization. I visualized this book even before we began writing it. I knew exactly how it would look, its size, thickness, how many chapters it would have, and how heavy it would feel in my hands. Visualization is a very powerful and effective tool. The more detailed and targeted your visuals are, the more effective they become.

For example, think of your favorite food, a bowl of hot tomato soup, a juicy fish fillet, a delicious muffin or a red velvet cake. As you read this just close your eyes for a second and visualize them. Did you start salivating? I know I am. I have this great urge to eat something sweet right now.

Visualizing stimulates the same parts of your brain that would have been affected by seeing, smelling, and tasting the real thing. What's more, if the visuals are appealing enough, your brain will subconsciously start working toward making this into a reality. You will soon start seeing positive signs, things rolling almost magically into place. This is called synchronicity, which can be defined as a "meaningful coincidence."

Your eyes gather all of the information from your surroundings, but the brain, being a super-efficient organ, doesn't process all of it. It filters out the irrelevant and only processes the important stuff. For example, let's say you were planning to buy a particular model car. Since this information is simmering somewhere in your subconscious, you will suddenly start seeing those cars everywhere. Now, of course, they'd been there all along, you just weren't aware of them. You may also start seeing great deals, or unexpected bargains and opportunities that you would have easily overlooked before.

By visualizing that car, you've created a clear goal for yourself. Your mind wants to fulfill that goal, to satisfy that desire.

The same is true of your CCIE. **Once you get your mind going towards a goal, through visualization, it starts looking for ways to achieve it**. It subconsciously starts steering you toward applicable articles in magazines, and websites, and toward knowledgeable people. You may even find yourself regularly, almost inexplicably, overhearing conversations involving the words "CCIE" or "lab" or "Cisco Certification."

If it helps, you can think of this process in terms of a network. What your brain is doing is opening a port that allows only certain information in; the rest is simply excluded, in the same way that a firewall might allow only HTTP or HTTPS traffic.

At one time or another, we have all been passed over for a promotion because we did not have the right qualifications. Instead of blaming your boss, or being jealous of your colleagues, you should use this to **fuel the fire of intention, and propel yourself toward the position of your desire**. If you want to be the team lead, you must learn to think like one. This can be accomplished through visualization. Here's how:

a. Visualize yourself as the team lead. How would you be expected to act?

b. As a lead, team members will come to you for advice. What questions would they ask? What questions have you asked of your lead? How did he or she address them? How would you address them?

c. You will be expected to lead discussions, nurture new projects, and provide all of the information anyone else needs. Think about how your current team leads do this. Would you do anything differently? Try to imagine some strategies that you'd like to implement or experiment with.

As you continue to use these visualization techniques, you will find that your behavior begins to change. You will find yourself thinking and acting like a team lead, which, in turn, will change, sometimes subtly, how your boss and coworkers perceive you. You'll have a better idea of what kind of questions or advice team members might need from you, and arm yourself with that knowledge. For example, let's say there are voice quality issues in your VoIP network. Through visualization, you might realize that you need to read more about Quality of Service (QoS), delay, jitter, and any other issue that might affect call quality. After you've done this, you can talk confidently about your analyses and answer any questions your boss and coworkers may have. Do this a couple of times and you will be *the go-to guy* in your organization.

If you continue to anticipate your team's needs, and can stay informed on all of the new and necessary technologies, your colleagues will solicit your advice for any problems they face. You will soon be the preferred candidate for a team lead. You will be assigned tasks, and the people around you will help you complete them.

Just by visualizing, you will be taking that first step forward, and will find yourself **going from one in the crowd, to the only one in the crowd.** And when you add your CCIE to it, a floodgate of opportunities will open to you. You will be able to choose what you want to work on, and how you want to make it happen. Your influence will increase ten-fold. Before you only participated in a project, now you will get to shape it.

What We Did (by Vivek)

To help us visualize, we updated our résumé with the words "CCIE (to be acquired May 2007)." This solidified our commitment to it, and made our résumés instantly more marketable.

We updated our future email signatures with a tentative CCIE number.

We prepared "thank you" emails for all of the congratulatory messages we would receive upon getting our CCIE.

Here is a personal example of the power of visualization, though not directly related to the CCIE.

When Video over IP was a new technology and being considered for a pilot program, I [(Vivek)] jumped in and volunteered to participate. This was a new technology, so only a few people had even heard about it. I was asked to read many dull manuals, and then evaluate the different products being pitched by the different vendors. To do this, I used the visualization techniques I had learned earlier. I imagined myself comparing the various video solutions, the possible difficulties in implementing them versus the possible rewards, and then being congratulated when the implementation was successful. To do this correctly, and with as much information as I could find, I found myself talking to the vendor sales engineers about the relative advantages of its products over its competitors. I did this with every sales engineer I encountered, and acquired quite a bit of information. I tabulated all of it into an Excel spreadsheet and created a very nice comparison chart.

I presented the chart to my boss, who was happy to have it. He presented it to the director. The director immediately called me into his office. He looked at my evaluation, and then asked me which one I recommended. He told me that call quality on the old equipment was not good, and that sometimes the call could not be established at all. This was affecting production network. I got as much information from him as I could about what management is looking for, and promised him an answer within a week.

Soon after that meeting, the operations manager started talking to me proactively about implementation. He wanted to know how much training his staff would need to maintain these new network devices. I promised to get that information as well.

All of this rolled like a snowball, and soon I was the only one with all of the knowledge about the Video over IP project. I found myself in meetings with decision makers, and they all knew me by my first name. They would stop me in the hallways to ask about our progress on the project. Personnel in other departments also approached me to see if theirs could be involved in the pilot project too.

Believe me, I was in visualization heaven. That's how I accomplished all of these tasks. I basically just visualized what information I was expected to have, what steps I needed to take to implement it successfully, and my brain unconsciously guided me toward that goal. I was "the go-to-guy" when it came to Video over IP, and after the pilot had been implemented, and was enormously successful, I became the go-to-guy of my boss and our director.

CHAPTER 12: THE THIRD KEY

All or Nothing

There's an interesting dichotomy between what we humans expect of other people (and things in life) and what we'll accept from ourselves. For instance, we expect our food to be cooked to our taste 100% of the time. We expect our electricity and our phone service to run uninterrupted 100% of the time. We expect the doctor to be able to cure our ailment or the police to catch a perpetrator 100% of the time. However, when it comes to our own activities, we're often content to lower our expectations. We might be happy with 99%, or 95%, sometimes even 75%. After all, 75% of perfect is a lot better than nothing at all, is it not?

But just imagine what would happen if pilots and doctors were held to the same standards. Would you be willing to trust your life to a pilot who was only careful 75% of the time? Would you submit to surgery at the hands of a doctor who was only willing to put in a half-hearted effort, so that he could get in time to watch the game?

Of course you wouldn't. But all too often, we find ourselves procrastinating, then doing an inadequate job, just to complete it as quickly as possible so that we can move on to something more interesting or engaging. In these instances, being thorough or meticulous gets thrown overboard.

The problem is, CCIE is one of the most difficult certifications that you can get. **It is a career-changing prospect, one that requires total commitment and painstaking attention to detail**, not just 75% of the time, nor even 99% of the time, but a full 100% of the time.

That's not to say that there aren't activities in life that you can't get away with giving less than 100%. Of course there are. CCIE however is not one of them.

A very successful boxing coach used to demand that his boxers make an effort to run (what is called "roadwork" in boxing) every day, without question. He explained to his boxers that he was preparing them for the unexpected, that you never knew if something was going to come up tomorrow that would prevent you from achieving your goal. And while you might not lose the endurance that roadwork provided by missing one day, you certainly would if you missed anymore.

If your effort is 95% or 99% then you have some wiggle room to postpone or have the chance of something else taking priority. We're not saying that you should stop everything else. After all, the lawn will still need to be mowed, and the dishes will still need to be done. What we are saying is that if you've allocated four hours every evening for study, you shouldn't let anything interfere with that. **<u>Giving 100% to your CCIE means that it has priority over everything else.</u>** If you have to sacrifice or postpone something, it should be the things that are lower priority. After all, that grass isn't going to stop growing, and it's not going anywhere, is it? You can easily defer doing that until a later date or during a study break.

After I ^(Vivek) earned my first CCIE, many engineers would joke with me, saying, "I wish I had a job that was easy enough so I could study for my CCIE too." I always told them that it didn't matter how difficult or time consuming my job was, I could always find time to study. Instead of going out to lunch, I'd say, I would just eat it at my desk while I was studying. It also doesn't take any extra time or effort to keep a to-do list of small topics or technical terms to study anytime you have a free moment. And in the course of my day, while working on different technologies, I'd just dig a little deeper into their operation and design. Not only did this help me in my quest for the CCIE, it allowed me to understand and do my job better.

What We Did (by Vivek)

When we began our quest, Dean and I decided that to be successful, the CCIE had to be our top priority. This meant it took precedence over birthdays, anniversaries, our children's dance recitals and sports events, as well as movies, TV, festivals, and social gatherings.

We made a list of all of the terms and technologies we didn't thoroughly understand. Whenever, we found some free time even fifteen minutes, we reviewed one of them. It's almost unbelievable how much you can get done fifteen minutes at a time, throughout the day. We did things like prepare configurations for future labs and lab diagrams. We'd print these out for reference or quick study. We'd also use those fifteen minute intervals to listen to audio, watch instructional Video-on-Demand (VoD) or check out options on a particular command on the Cisco web page. We would always ask ourselves **"What can we do in the next fifteen minutes that will take us closer to our CCIE?"**

CHAPTER 13: UNLOCK THE BOX

The Three-Key Combination

Over the course of the last few chapters, we have given you the keys to success. Now we are going to show you how to put them all together in a way that will help you pass the CCIE exams and acquire that coveted number.

To illustrate this, I [(Vivek)] am going to tell you a little story.

When I was a kid, I was fascinated by bank safety deposit boxes and how they operated. I liked, especially, how they were always located inside a huge vault. Stepping into it was like entering a large safe. The walls were made of eight to ten inches of solid steel and the bolts were these huge shiny cylinders that slid into their recesses, which made the room virtually impenetrable without the proper key or combination. Once inside, it seemed even more clandestine and mysterious. The banker came in with his key, and you had your key, and you needed both of them, turned almost in tandem, to open the safety deposit box.

To access your safety deposit box **there were three keys that were essential**.

1. The key or the combination to the vault.

2. Your key to the safety deposit box.

3. Bankers key to the safety deposit box.

   With these three keys your access to the contents of the safety deposit box happened with little effort. But even if **one of the keys was missed there is no way you could access** the contents.

The previous three chapters are like your keys to the safety deposit box that has your CCIE number. Success becomes a lot easier and assured if you use these keys.

1. Setting your goal.

2. Visualizing your goal.

3. Give it your 100%.

If you don't **use all of these keys together and in tandem** the safety deposit box will not open.

CHAPTER 14: LET THE GAMES BEGIN!

So you decided to do your CCIE, now what?

You should be proud of yourself for starting this endeavor. You must remember, though, that the ultimate goal is not just to pass an exam; **it's to get your CCIE number.** This may seem counter-intuitive at first, since you must pass an exam before you can get your CCIE number, but it's all about training your brain. You see, when you set your CCIE number as your goal, the exam becomes just one more step in the process. In this way, not passing the exam becomes merely a minor setback—one bump in the road rather than a roadblock. Your brain seeks to fulfill your goals, and if the goal is to pass the lab and you don't, your mind interprets this as a failure. However, if the goal is to get your CCIE number, your mind will work on it until you get it.

You can get a good idea of what you need to read and what books to use as a reference on Cisco's website, CCIE blueprint. I [Dean] would also suggest that you spend some time researching CCIE training providers. Contact them directly and ask if they offer any special promotions. Who knows, you may get a good discount. When looking for the right training provider, keep in mind they should have the most up to date program relating to Cisco's latest exam format. For instance, they should be able to guide you on how to handle the troubleshooting section of the exam, how to answer open ended questions, or make you aware of any upcoming changes in the lab exam. You should also talk to as many other engineers as possible. Find out what strategies worked best for them, and what potential pitfalls might await you.

Once you've decided on a CCIE training provider and a program, you should stick with it. Each CCIE training provider offers a variety of programs to suit different learning styles and various CCIE tracks. Jumping from one to the other could disrupt the flow and cause confusion. **The most important thing to understand at this point is that there are no shortcuts**. In the end, you must learn the content and complete the practice labs. Think of it this way: in order to gain muscle, you've got to lift weights. No one can do that for you. However, a good trainer can help you gain muscle faster--and more effectively--by focusing your exercise routine. Imagine your CCIE training provider as the trainer in the CCIE Olympics gym and your goal is to get the CCIE medal (which is your own CCIE number). Your courseware should tell you, in great detail, about all of the technical aspects, but your training provider will help you maximize the results.

We feel that within two weeks of signing up with the training provider of your choice, you should have your study routine, hardware, and software for the lab. If you are using router simulator, such as DYNAMIPS and GNS3, you should also have a powerful computer. Now it's time to choose a timeline. Look at the different timeline schedules at the end of this book for guidance. Regardless of which timeline you choose, set the first target date to check your progress at about four weeks. Based on the progress made in these four weeks, you should decide if you want to follow the study time line you have already chosen. This is also a good time to customize your study timeline. We do not recommend changing your study schedule after this point. Check the CCIE actual lab availability and adjust your schedule accordingly. Remember that the lab dates during certain times of the year (especially during and after holidays) are harder to get. Some engineers who are ready to take the lab exam check availability multiple times a day for any last minute cancellations.

CHAPTER 15: YOUR PARTNER IN SUCCESS

Choose wisely

Your study partner is a significant part of your CCIE Lab preparation process. Though there are people who prefer to work independently, we have noticed that the majority of successful candidates had study partners; after all you don't know the answer to everything and having someone else to ask questions is truly invaluable. Having a study partner also makes you a better learner, through the ability to discuss any questions that either one of you may have. It is a proven fact that when accomplishing a challenging task, working with a partner benefits both partners, providing them with an ability to see something from another person's point of view and approach the problem differently. Besides, teaching is learning. Selecting a study partner depends on numerous factors including, but not limited to personality, study habits, location and technical background. You want to choose a partner to compliment your strengths and assist in your weaknesses.

In our experience having at least one or a maximum of two partners is sufficient. Having more minds looking at a problem can get it resolved faster. It also helps you when you have more questions about a specific technology. Usually you will be strong in certain technologies while your partner may be strong in others. This complements your study and a team effort will speed up your work.

It would be a good idea to look for these qualities in your study partner.

1. They should be of similar experience and intelligence levels. We are not saying to get an IQ test, but if you are answering all of the questions and not getting your questions answered it is not going to last long.

2. Your knowledge of technologies should complement each other.

3. Personalities and temperaments should be taken into account.

4. Your partner should bring a positive attitude and be part of the solution and not the problem. You want to work with someone who sees the glass half full and not half empty.

5. It is important to choose a study partner who can make a commitment to devote their time until the completion of the certification. Dropping a partner midway disrupts the flow and equilibrium that you have established and may disturb your progress and time of completion.

6. Your partner should be approachable and available at any hour, in

the same time zone and it is highly preferable that he is in the same location so that you are able to study together face to face.

7. Your partner should have the same time schedule at least on the weekends when you would be studying together.

8. You and your partner should be able to complete the tasks that you have assigned to yourselves for that week.

9. Your partner will be one that can push you to finish one more task in the lab or work on the next attempt and help you answer your questions. **Partners are there to be supportive and to ensure that you don't quit.**

10. You also need to make sure that you keep this in mind; if you choose a study partner who has already scheduled his lab for two weeks from now and you haven't started any practice labs, then that partnership will not be beneficial.

We emphasize again that these are not rules but just guidelines to follow. Every engineer has his own unique situations and expectations.

What We Did (by Vivek)

Dean and I are very competitive individuals and as we mentioned previously, we wanted to see who could get his CCIE certification first. We complemented each other when it came to technologies. For example, Dean

is strong in MPLS while I am strong in QoS.

We divided any new technologies that we both had to learn and each one

would present his portion. We would quiz each other and ask questions to

ensure the concept was fully understood.

We even used sarcasm and comic relief at times to point out each

other's weaknesses. There was an instance when Dean called me to say

that after five hours into the lab he could not get anything working. I called

him an unrepeatable name, and unknown to me, Dean was upset and

decided to work through the night and started the lab from scratch. To my

surprise at 4AM my cell phone was ringing and it was Dean stating he had

completed the lab, he knew what he was doing and did not want to be

called that irritating—and unrepeatable—name anymore. All of this was of

course done in a very healthy way. We liked to taunt each other and never

took anything personally—this worked out for both of us. Although a few

years have gone by since we got our CCIEs, we are still in touch and are now

working together again in writing this book.

CHAPTER 16: PRACTICE HARD AND PLAY EVEN HARDER

Study aggressively with your goal in sight

In our personal opinion, the best way to approach CCIE certification is to have an aggressive plan. **Work hard to make sure that you are executing your plan.** If you drag your goal, after a few weeks, you will realize that it is harder to get back on track and soon it feels like your goal is too large and you begin to procrastinate and give up.

Cisco provides you with an overwhelming amount of resources; the CCIE lab blue print has a big list of books and topics that are recommended for reading. Everything that is on the test is probably listed there. However, if you want to get your CCIE quickly you don't have the luxury of reading the entire content. That is where the lab guides and the boot camps from your training provider come into play. They let you channel your limited resources to your full potential and, laser like; you will focus on the topics that do matter in the lab exam.

We have compiled five different strategic timelines for five different scenarios to assist you in navigating the appropriate path for you. Keep in mind that, these timelines are generic and may not necessarily be a perfect fit for you and your study partner. These give you a starting point on which you can adjust and build your own timeline. See Chapter 37 "Suggested Timelines for CCIE Preparation."

As we discussed our success strategy and compared it with other CCIE tracks, it was clear to us that once you have one CCIE, your timeline for the second CCIE will be shorter. This is because of the following four factors.

1) Usually engineers go with CCIE tracks that have some basic common elements. For example, if you start with R&S (routing and switching) the odds are that you may go to Service Provider or Security since it builds on the previous track.

2) Similarities in exam blueprints, for example, if you know your BGP for IPv4 address-family, then learning VPNv4 address-family will not be as intensive as learning the entire protocol suit from scratch.

3) Now that you have been through one CCIE you know your study habits, how to find time and how to concentrate and work for long hours.

4) You are much more patient as you are now aware that CCIE is a long term commitment.

Point being, that for your next CCIE your timeline is substantially shorter. It also depends on your knowledge base and the amount of exposure that you have had at work or in a lab environment.

After we successfully passed our CCIE certification, one of our friends approached us for advice on how to study and the kinds of strategies we used to pass the exam. We basically gave him a quick approach to what we did; a simplified version of this book. This friend got motivated, loved the advice and decided to study and pass the exam. Since then, whenever we meet up with him, he would tell stories about something that stopped him in his studies. On a somewhat annual basis, he still is asking the same question and soliciting our advice for his CCIE Lab exam. He starts studying, but then many factors slow him down and he stops and then has to renew his written certification again to qualify for the lab exam. After four years, of our friend going through the same cycle, we told him that **without showing 100% commitment, success would be nearly impossible: do something**, don't let excuses get in your way. Chapter 10, 11 and 12 talk about what he was missing.

What We Did (by Dean)

For our first CCIE track, we did not have a specific timeline or a plan to follow. We knew we had to study hard, improvise and not give up. For our second CCIE track, we came up with a specific timeline and worked diligently to achieve every milestone.

We are providing you with our five strategic timelines, so you can select whichever is appropriate for you. Use them as a frame of reference and customize this to create a personalized timeline that suits your needs and more fitting to your abilities.

If you have other suggestions or recommendations that you would like to share, please visit our website www.2doubleccies.com and post your comments to: contact@2doubleccies.com.

CHAPTER 17: MAKE A SCHEDULE, AND WORK THE SCHEDULE

Schedule your study hours

Make a schedule and work the schedule. If you have already planned your study schedule, you have to stick to it and if you miss a day or two you may find it hard to get back on track. Don't let it slide; get back on track and start working the schedule until it becomes a habit. Regardless of what anyone does, you need to find your own suitable timelines that work best for you, your family and your study partner.

If you are a night owl, then make sure to start your routine every weekday on time, as if you are going to work. This is your second job for now.

As a part of our schedule, we made sure to have a primary and backup place to study. In the U.S., libraries are a great place to study. They even have study rooms where you can discuss and work on your lab. Other places such as coffee shops, your home office, and local college or university campuses could also be considered.

What We Did (by Vivek)

For Dean, who had young children during his second CCIE, he decided that his lab time would be from 8PM to 1AM on weekdays. The children would go to sleep and then he could easily devote all of his attention to the lab without any distractions.

During the weekends, we did not find it conducive to study at home, because there was so much going and the distractions were unavoidable. We decided to go to our local office, which is about half hour away, to continue our studying routine. We stayed there from 9AM to 7 PM and even until 11PM at times. We sustained this schedule until we were satisfied that we had covered a sufficient amount of content, to the point that we could work independently; this took about four months. During those months, every Saturday and Sunday rain or shine, sleet or snow; we studied. We studied the videos, attempted the labs, and reviewed any topics that we needed to improve upon.

After four months, when we were content with our progress, we knew that neither of us would be stopping until we earned our second CCIE. The motivation, dedication, and continued support from our families made us devote longer hours into this project.

Subsequently, we were independently working on our schedule and continued our regular daily calls to check on each other's progress. If one of us had a technical issue, either lunch hour or evening time, we were both jumping on the problem until we resolved the issue and recognized the root cause. After all, this was our battle and neither of us could be silent when the other had a problem to overcome; we were truly a tag-team partnership. The urge to continue to reach our goal was overpowering. On a daily basis, we would complete one full lab, and our focus was laser like. At times, we would sit for six hours and finish any practice lab and felt confident that it worked.

CHAPTER 18: THE TICKING CLOCK

Time is a resource. How to use it, how to find it

One of the most important resources that you have to manage during the CCIE lab preparation is your time. After having your family on board, (see Chapter 7 "The circle of trust"), you may want to talk to your boss about this endeavor. Many times at companies such as Cisco and its partners, or large service providers, the department and the management team would get recognized by having CCIEs on their staff. Ensure your boss is your advocate and allows you more time for preparation and to request flexible working hours during these months of preparation.

Once your family and your boss are on board, **it is a matter of planning, sheer grit and determination to use this time and these resources to achieve your goal.**

As mentioned earlier, you may have to re-prioritize your goals and as well as your time that you would have spent for other activities, such as watching TV. One of the things that I [Vivek] always ask my family and friends is how many hours do you spend watching TV? Most of them don't even realize that they are spending more time in front of a box than they realize. Point being, you need to manage your time and always focus your efforts.

Think, **"How does this activity help with my CCIE certification?"** If it is not directly related, you may want to cut or reconsider the amount of time put into it.

We all have our routines and it seems impossible to devote so much time to studying. Time is available, but are you using it to your advantage? How do you get thirty or forty hours in one week when you already have a family, full time job or taking care of others?

From our experience and the interviews that we had with successful CCIEs, including those with multiple CCIE's under their belt, we found that you have to find the best time that you feel ready, alert and have minimal distractions. One individual told me that he starts his morning at 3AM and does lab work until 7AM. This gives him four hours of studying time before the family wakes up. In a regular workweek, he can accumulate twenty hours of studying. On the weekend, if he completes one full eight-hour lab, he has put in twenty eight hours in one week. He could also find more time by staying back at work (after hours) and study for that time.

Feed the CCIE animal in you and leverage your time accordingly. For example, manage your commute to avoid the rush hour and instead use that time to practice small labs, study a Video-on-Demand (VoD). You may do all of the prep work for your studies in the morning, and then prepare yourself during lunchtime to do some work in the evening. Regardless, if there is a will, you will need to find the way. You need to create your own study schedule and make it suit your needs.

You need to use every free moment to your advantage. Therefore, we recommend that you print out information (flash cards, articles and configurations) to be available within arm's reach and review it, as soon as you find fifteen minutes or more time available. You may also want to have Audio-on-Demand (AoD) or VoD available to you on your laptop or on your smart phone so that you can watch and/or listen any time. For example, you are going to your child's game and it will be a thirty minute drive; bring along few pages about a topic that you need to ramp up on or listen to on the drive over. Doing this will enable you to use your time wisely. You may be surprised to find that you are able to grasp a new or difficult concept. You want to be just like a child with a new video game. All of his time is spent playing. He is steadfast in his ambition and concentration of the game. A child will play and focus every waking moment of the day on the game and everything else is just a distraction—this is how your passion for CCIE should be.

The above approach has one caution; **don't sacrifice your sleep or your health**. If you want to have effective and fruitful results, then get your rest.

If your body needs seven hours of sleep then give it time to rejuvenate and heal itself. The worst thing that you can do is to wake up tired, cranky, and ineffective and get on others' nerves. I used to have a colleague who bragged about only needing three hours of sleep, but every morning at our 6AM meeting we had to deal with his bad temper and out-of-control attitude as he tried and wanted to pick a fight with the vendors, us and even the customer; which didn't go well.

What We Did (by Vivek)

Once our routine was established, we used to wake up in the morning without an alarm and would practice our lab or start a new setup. Both of us found that morning hours were the best for dealing with challenging topics. That would be when we could focus the most and we knew we could grasp the technology that we had a hard time with the night before. There were instances when Dean, or I, woke up to a much better understanding of a concept that we struggled with on the previous nights.

CHAPTER 19: BOOKS/VIDEOS/LAB RESOURCES

Use of training options

Once you endeavor to take the CCIE, you have to first think of your learning style. Each of us has a different learning strategy. You need to know which learning resource works the best for you and how to master it. It is imperative for you to spend some time to research available resources, tools, equipment, simulation and place of study. Choose the ones that are most advantageous to your learning style and then visualize yourself reading, or listening and learning the contents on the medium of your choice. **Good research will take you a long way.** Any experienced project manager can testify to the importance of planning. It is one of the most important steps in any project and can encompass more time than other processes.

See how these training courses and lab books match your studying style. For example, if you go to CCIE blueprint they have recommended readings. If your intent is on reading all of these books, you may not remember the first book by the time you have finished the tenth one. Most likely, you may have forgotten some important technical details that you picked up in the first book, especially when you are just reading them without any hands-on or practical experience. Many people consider technical books to be dry. You may consider them as sleeping pills because they will put you to sleep after a few pages—yes that would be Dean who feels this way!

The training resources available to us today range from an intense boot camp course, live online education, Video On Demand (VoD), Audio on Demand (AoD), instructor led courses, seminars, as well as Cisco Live Sessions geared towards the various certification tracks. Although you may want to do all of the above, you need to plan and **stick with one major training provider** and use other options as additional supplements in achieving your goal. In other words, don't stretch yourself too thin as this will overwhelm you. In our personal opinion, many items such as books, AoD, VoD and lectures are great resources and should be used on an as-needed basis. I have seen engineers use VoD for their initial training and then go to a week-long boot camp just a few weeks before their actual lab attempt.

Please keep in mind that your objective is not based on how many books you have completed from cover to cover or how many hours you have put into this certification! But rather, **your objective is getting that CCIE number**. You will pass the test by practicing as many labs as you can.

Instead of memorizing the practice labs **understand the concepts**

behind each lab. The confidence that you generate after completing a few of these practice labs successfully will be the catalyst for your success. The bottom line is that you should be doing this to get your CCIE number and everything else should be considered as means towards that goal.

What We Did (by Vivek)

For our second CCIE certification, we both had a solid understanding of certain protocols, so we decided to focus on the areas that we had to ramp-up on. We decided to start with VoD. After first watching the videos, we started taking time-stamped notes of the VoD and simulated each segment of the lab using all of the resources that we had (See Chapter 20 "VoD" for details). The purpose of this approach was two-fold; first, to validate our knowledge base as well as the accuracy of video lectures and secondly, to correct any issues, mistakes that the video lecturer may have made or ones that we made ourselves.

Once the technical concept was fully understood, it was time for hands-on practice. We started by simulating the short labs, which cover a lesson on a particular technology. A majority of these labs build on top of each other, so all we had to do was look at the most complicated lab. With this lab topology created on our simulator, we mimicked the earlier labs (the least complicated ones) by turning off interfaces that were not needed. Once the lab was fully functional, each of us took turns to practicing and troubleshooting. Another thing to remember is that if you get stuck at a certain place, you can save that scenario and restart or move ahead to the next lab. After each lab, we had a conference call to discuss the lessons learned and to share any ideas or alternative solutions that we may have thought of during these extensive exercises. We pressed each other to complete these labs. Once we were satisfied with our results, we then moved to the longer four-hour labs.

CHAPTER 20: VOD

How to exploit Video's On Demand

There are many learning resources available, but we preferred Video-on-Demand (VoD). Why? Because, we liked the visual format and were able to learn at our own pace and go back and forth. If you also choose to take the VoD option, we have some helpful advice.

At the onset, create the same network being used in the VoD on your simulator or lab. As you are listening to the VoD, make note of the time when a particular topic starts and stops. This will let you to go back to the same point to review. This is a huge timesaver and allows you to learn new technologies effectively.

Here is <u>**a four-step process that we used to ensure that we had**</u> <u>**mastered the Video-on-Demand**</u>:

<u>Step 1:</u> Watch and listen to one complete video, and understand the basic concepts.

<u>Step 2:</u> Now start the video again, this time pause taking detailed notes on the topics you think you may be weak on, or will need to review.

<u>Step 3:</u> Using your notes, simulate the VoD network in your lab. Hands on experience reinforces and crystallizes the whole topic into your brain.

<u>Step 4:</u> Go back to Video on Demand, and this time validate, and compare the VoD with your work. This way, you will be able to catch any of the mistakes that you have made.

You may still have a few questions, but those can be answered by reading a book, or through training provider forums. You can also ask your partner or colleagues.

This process is tedious but works very well. At the outset, it may take longer, but will save you a lot of time later on. To get your partner involved, go to an environment where you will be able to talk, watch the videos together and show your work.   Being in the same room with your study partner is much more productive than studying remotely. Expect the learning from Video-on-Demand to take time, especially if you are not in the same room, at which time you can use web based sharing technologies to coordinate your work.

We have seen other engineers who have taken elaborate notes with use of hyperlinks, PDF content, and other reference points. This comprehensive and sophisticated knowledge-base is splendid if you can keep up with the milestones on your timeline.

Try using different methods and technologies in your lab by using the question mark in the commands. Use various options and see the effect.

This will help you a lot in learning the features and will also enable you to answer those tricky questions or come up with workarounds as you make your way through the lab. Breaking what you are doing also helps you when you are troubleshooting.

What We Did (by Dean)

We utilized the Video on Demand approach for learning technologies to the fullest possible extent. We spent a lot of time on this initially because we had not yet formulated our four-step approach. For our CCIE lab exam preparation, we watched the VoD independently. Then, each of us went through the videos making detailed notes with time stamps. Later on, if we had to refer back to a certain section of a VoD, we did not have to watch the entire video again. Remember, it looks easy when the instructor is typing and making technologies work, but when you start the labs on the routers yourself, it is difficult to remember the exact steps without any reference. Therefore, it is imperative that you follow steps three and four to recreate the same topology on the simulator or lab (hands on). For us, a forty hour class took about three to four weeks to finish.

We used the question mark to find out what additional options were available or options that we may have ignored. Using the question mark enabled us to see what other parameters could be manipulated.

We were always probing what other scenarios could be possible using a particular command option. After we completed this exercise, each of us broke the lab and had the other person work on it; this helped immensely with our troubleshooting technique. The more ways you know how to break it the easier it will be for you to troubleshoot it.

There were times, while watching the Video, when we knew that the instructor was wrong. Since we ran the scenario in our lab, we were able to determine the root cause of the problem. It was informative to watch the instructor, correct his mistakes as well as how he troubleshot. We firmly believe that the time we invested in learning these videos initially helped us immensely in achieving our goal.

CHAPTER 21: LEARN THE STROKES

Use of short labs to learn a specific technology

Almost all of the CCIE lab-training providers have different resources available for you when you buy your training bundles; short labs are a part of this. These labs are simple setups of three to five devices that focus on one technology. These series, of short labs build on each other; from a simple to a more complicated network.   Studying and practicing on <u>the</u> **<u>short labs will enable you to understand the technologies, and provides</u>** **<u>you with this new sense of confidence</u>**. This is because you will have hands on experience and will be able to test the various options that are available to you.

After completing the short labs you may want to read the eight-hour practice labs that you just purchased and fairly assess yourself, including the level of your technical skills. If you feel that you do not have any problems on the core technologies of the exam (which is 60 to 70%), then go ahead and attempt it.   However, if you think that there are a few of these technologies that you need to dig deeper into, please wait before doing the complete eight-hour labs. Digging deeper is easy; use the above mentioned technology specific short labs.

What We Did (by Dean)

During our second CCIE studies, we used the short practice labs to familiarize ourselves with the various technologies. We simulated any technology that we felt we were weak on, or needed to review. We looked at the short labs and created a set up that we could use for the entire section. Lab setup can take some time so we completed it in off study hours, such as our lunch break at work. This way it ensured that we could concentrate only on learning during our study hours.

Once we knew the individual technologies and built our confidence, we were then ready to take on the longer practice labs.

CHAPTER 22: MAINTAIN YOUR FORM

How to keep healthy

When you start spending long hours preparing for CCIE Lab exam, there are changes that will happen to your body. Weight gain is one factor. Don't forget you are sitting behind a computer on a daily basis, sometimes for over ten to fifteen hours a day. Expect it and don't stress out over it.

Let's **keep your mind sharp and your body healthy** during this stressful period of about 12 months. One good approach to manage stress is to exercise regularly. Perhaps doing some Yoga, Tai-chi or other meditation movement will clear your mind. I [(Dean)] often practice yoga by following a series of videos and doing them any time I feel overwhelmed with work or am under any sort of stress. Others have stated that doing cardiovascular movement would increase blood flow to your brain and get your heart pumping.

During lab preparation, I was getting tired, and found myself unable to focus at times. So I took an old friend's advice and started doing twenty pushups and twenty sit-ups multiple times in a day. Though it was hard at first and I could manage only ten each time with three rotations daily; to my surprise, I found that I was getting a quick workout in minutes and it gave me a boost and a fast heartbeat. I felt motivated without taking an extensive break or calling it a day. After the short exercise routine, I was ready to focus and continue with the lab. I repeated this every time I was tired. Eventually I started doing three sets of thirty in a day. I start with one set first thing in the morning and the remaining sets done during my study period. This also helped with backaches that I was getting by sitting down for so many hours in front of a computer screen.

Within a month, I was well into my exam preparation working out as I studied. Many times, when I wanted to get motivated, I would drop to the floor and attempt thirty to forty pushups. Within minutes, I was back on track and my mind was as sharp as it could be.

Give this a try if you can (but please take your physician's advice in case you have any health issues-this is what worked for us); once you get hooked on this exercise routine you may want to continue even after you pass CCIE exam. By the way, this routine doesn't require any machines or club memberships or any additional cost to your CCIE budget. So you can do this anytime and anywhere you feel appropriate, just avoid doing this in public areas as you may be getting some extra unwanted attention. With regular workouts, you can have a CCIE *and* a six pack ☺.

What We Did (by Dean)

As I mentioned before, you are subjecting your body, mind and family to stress that you may not have faced before. As a result, you may start eating more or develop new unhealthy habits. In my case, I started eating a lot of junk food that resulted in me gaining weight. This happens. It varies for different people, but the key here is to be aware of this and know how to deal with it. Give yourself a break often, especially when you feel overwhelmed. In order to build our stamina and mental focus, we started eating healthier; by bringing fruits and vegetables to our weekend study location instead of the usual coffee and donuts.

Do not sweat it if you fall off the wagon with your diet, or miss your regular food and exercise routine at times. You will be able to get back on your old routine once you have the CCIE, and can tighten your belt later!!

Another factor that you need to take into consideration is your environment and that it is suitable for your needs. You need to make sure that you are free from distractions, noises, and that the temperature is comfortable. We found the best environment was in our local office. On weekends, there were no disturbances since nobody would be there. It was nicely lit and had ergonomic furniture in familiar surroundings. Plus we had a projector to watch and analyze our technical VoD on a big screen. Many times when we decided to take a quick break, Dean started his workout

routine of pushups and sit-ups.

Checkout our videos at

www.2doubleccie.com

CHAPTER 23: DO MORE TO GET MORE

How to push your partner

Now that we have looked at the criteria to select a partner (Chapter 15: "Your partner in Success"), it's important for you to also look at personalities. Many engineers, though great with technologies, may be lacking personal skills (though it is hard for us to admit!). Remember that your study partner is there to call upon you for support and you should be able to do the same.

From our point of view, you are the project manager for this endeavor and communication is 90% of the task of any good manger. Make sure that both of you are kept in the loop because there will be many issues that may arise during the few months of studying, whether they be personal, professional or motivational.

<u>Push yourself, and push your partner(s) everyday,</u> and as many times a day as needed. You should know exactly what their strengths and weaknesses are. Use their strengths to help yourself and support them on their weaknesses. You should leverage each other's positive attributes to complete this common goal.

Vivek and I [(Dean)] used to keep track of each other's activities and daily progress made, and shared the lessons learned. We also divided the questions that we had among ourselves. On our next meeting, we would come prepared and were ready to teach our selected topics. They say teaching is learning, and we learned something every day through this exercise.

With a long term project like the CCIE Lab, a tight schedule, and constant pressure, it is human nature that setbacks will make you procrastinate or feel like giving up. You and your partner should motivate, compliment and pick up the slack. Please note that if you or your partner is always needy or is constantly looking for excuses not to do a fair share of the work, then you should reconsider this partnership.

What We Did (by Dean)

Regular daily communication between you and your study partner is a must. I remember Vivek calling me at 9:30AM, 1:30PM, 3:30PM and 5:30PM on Sunday, demanding to see how much I had accomplished and why the assigned lab was not complete. I would feel bad and start my lab at 9:30PM and not stop until 3:45AM. Vivek also had a nickname for me, which he granted one alphabet at a time when one or both of us had to accomplish a major task. By the time I got my second CCIE the complete title was given to me, "Sensei". With all seriousness, push yourself and your partner so you can finish. Once you get your CCIE, you will never have to look at this process and will most likely never have to go through the lab exam again. ☺

CHAPTER 24: CORE SHOULD BE UP 100%

Even the best car won't run if the engine fails.

As you progress into your CCIE lab study, you will understand what I
(Vivek) mean when I say that the core should be up 100%. Each CCIE lab has its
own core technologies that are its basis. For example, at the time we took
our CCIE Routing and Switching lab, the blue print had some of the core
technologies like switching, trunking, VLANS, routing protocols and their
redistribution. **These comprised the foundation of the network you would
build.** Once the core network is configured, the lab exam would add more
complexity on top. There will be IPv6, its routing protocols, multicast, QoS
and other topics covered in the lab exam. Unless basic end to end
connectivity is established, as per the parameters and conditions prescribed
in the lab, any other technology that builds on this network will not work.

A good analogy to this would be the functionality and productivity of a
city. If your city does not have properly built roads, traffic will not be able
to reach its desired destinations. It does not matter how much you spend on
an automatic traffic control system, since a good traffic control system
works only on good roads. Once your roads are suitable and traffic has
multiple paths to move from one place to the other, you can start building

car pool lanes.

This might sound trivial here but so many engineers get stuck at the core itself and the result is that all additional work becomes inconsequential. The core portion of the lab is about 60% to 70% of the exam and, therefore, you will require 30% to 40% more to pass. These numbers vary depending on which CCIE track you choose and any changes made by Cisco.

Your strength in the core technologies will also prepare you to troubleshoot issues that may/will arise while working on the actual CCIE Lab exam.

What We Did (by Vivek)

I clearly remember that on my second attempt I had completed the lab on time. Only one corner of the network (one router) was not forming neighbor adjacencies. I thought that this was a task with a very small number of points and everything else was working, so I left that to the end. By the end, since I was convinced that I had at least 90 plus points working, I did not bother to correct that. To my surprise, I failed. I was unbelievably disappointed. I went over the lab scenario in my mind again and again and that was the only part that I could think could be the reason for failing.

Needless to say, I was extra careful from then on for all my tasks.

From then on, for every actual lab exam that I took and passed, I was confident that I had completed the core 100% accurately.

CHAPTER 25: JUMPING INTO THE POOL

Do labs as if they are a real lab.

When astronauts want to practice their spacewalk activities they dress up in their special space suits and go into a customized pool. This pool simulates the zero gravity environment and has an exact replica of the object that they are supposed to be working. The astronauts use actual tools and simulate the work that they will be doing up in space. They practice different "what if" scenarios for months. This simulation and hard work makes the real work hanging upside down in space, travelling at a few hundred miles per hour feel like just another repetition of what they had already done dozens of times. Simulations can make you successful in your CCIE Lab as well.

In our experience, engineers start doing labs from their lab book piecemeal, which is the way to go initially. However, after completing the first six or seven full eight-hour practice labs in a piece by piece fashion, **do the next set of labs as if they were real; meaning completing in one sitting.** Keep in mind that if this is your first time attempting the practice labs, it may take you twice as long, if not longer. You may feel overwhelmed, but don't give up; this is a crucial part of the process.

In our work life, we are not used to sitting fully focused on one task for eight hours. **CCIE lab requires razor sharp focus, complete concentration and being in a state of heightened alert for the full eight-hours.** You must be able to master these skills in order to think fast, troubleshoot, configure, and validate if the configurations are working as requested in the lab. You have to verify, after every major section, that your newer configurations did not break any previous ones. You have to be able to build and troubleshoot on a network that is absolutely unfamiliar to you in a very short period of time. There is no outside help available aside from your own mind and Cisco documentation.

Try this: Select one of the full eight-hour practice labs that you have completed recently and time yourself from start to finish. This will give you a good idea regarding your speed and ability to focus. Do not get frustrated if it takes you more than ten hours. The very fact that you were able to complete a full lab in a span of ten or eleven hours is a big achievement. In the event that you are able to complete the lab in five to six hours, you are probably in very good shape. You may even want to consider scheduling your actual lab soon.

What We Did (by Vivek)

After I [(Vivek)] completed all of the short labs, I started working on the eight-hour practice labs. Within a few weeks of working on all of the eight-hour labs, I felt myself having the confidence to complete any one of them. I then scheduled a rental rack from a company that rented time on real physical equipment. Just as the astronauts used their pool, this was my pool now. I had my wife choose one lab at random and started it at about 8 AM. This was my first lab in my non-simulator environment. I was somewhat nervous as I thought of this as a real test.

The first three hours were good and things were going fine. Every time I finished a question, I wrote the time on the lab sheet that I had printed, and my score. In the fourth hour, I slowed down, as things were not working as predicted. By the end of the fourth hour it was lunch time and I reloaded all of my routers.

When I came back after lunch, my network was a mess. Quick troubleshooting told me that I had not saved the configuration on one of the routers. Now I had to think back and see what I was missing, which took forty-five minutes. I was under pressure and found myself working even faster than before to complete the lab on time and started making more mistakes. By the sixth hour, I was typing one router command into another and so on. It was a disaster. Everything stopped working; I could not even complete the lab in the ten and a half hours that I had scheduled the rack time for. This was very disappointing and a big eye opener for me. In that one day, I went from 80% confidence, to 30% confidence in my CCIE lab exam.

I tried the same lab after a few days and this time I was saving my configuration regularly but, by the sixth hour, I was again creating problems for myself and was stumped. Once again, I could not complete my lab in ten and a half hours. I was improving, but was not even close to being ready.

As I was doing these labs, I was making typing mistakes, and after three hours, I was losing my concentration. For example, after working on a problem and not being able to troubleshoot the issue, it finally occurred to me that I had spent forty-five minutes on the wrong device. I had to remove all of my configurations, correct my mistakes and do that particular section in the correct router.

I was trying again and again, only to face failure after failure. It became almost impossible to continue. After my fifth attempt, something happened. Everything just changed. I found myself having more concentration and was more focused than before. As a result, the core of my lab was up and running flawlessly in three hours and I was partially done with my redistribution by lunchtime. I was puzzled on some issues, but used Cisco documentation and kept on going. I finally completed my lab, tallied my points, and had at least 85 points out of 100 in ten hours. Although I was two hours over the time, I was overjoyed because something inside told me that I was close and everything was going smoothly. The problems I faced were a result of my misinterpretation of the questions, not my lack of understanding of the technology. It was quite a surreal experience as I was shut out from the world around me and was gliding through what I was doing. I repeated that again and again with more Labs so that I would be ready for my ultimate test. However, did I pass on my first attempt? You know the answer.

CHAPTER 26: EXPECT LOOSE ENDS

You may miss 5% to 7%.

We want you to know that there is a good chance you may not be able to complete all of the tasks in the actual lab. This is not necessarily due to time constraints, but rather to the nature of this lab exam. The topics for technologies and their features are so vast and very difficult to read and understand in a short period of time. That is the reason for this chapter. No matter how hard we tried, there were portions of the actual lab that had a small number of points that we could not attempt in spite of having about 30 minutes to spare. Though we had a good grasp of how to search for Cisco documentation in the lab (manually) we still could not find some of the relevant answers. If this happens to you, no need to panic. Make sure that your core technologies are working smoothly. **<u>Keep a tally of your points with every task you complete</u>**. Clarify with your proctor if you get points for a task that is partially working. If a task has three parts, A, B, and C and only A and B are working, then will you get credit for A and B, or will you only get a credit if all three are working? In our time it was all or nothing. Either you get credit for A, B and C, or you don't get any credit at all.

<u>**Read the CCIE Lab exam carefully**</u> as the answers to the above may be embedded in there.

Although the number of points required to pass the lab exam may be a bit lower than 90% you should aim for 90% to 95% if possible. This will take care of any errors or omissions that may happen unknowingly.

Cisco does a good job of updating the actual lab exams with current technologies and labs are continuously evolving. Please read the policy well in advance of taking the actual lab in order to ensure that you are well aware of any changes.

Practice your navigational skills for a manual search of Cisco documentation for a particular technology. This practice may give you that extra leverage of 5% to 10% on the CCIE Lab. Believe me the last 5% to 10% is very crucial and may make the difference between you passing the CCIE lab or not. Get to know the documentation tool very well as your passing depends on it.

What We Did (by Vivek)

When I [(Vivek)] did my actual lab exam, I kept a running tally of my points. In my tally, I counted those points that I was sure of and those that I was unsure of in two separate columns. The unsure portion was the one that would have contributed to my failure. The points that I was unsure of meant that I had to ramp up on those technologies and break them down. In almost every lab, I could not complete a small portion, because I was unfamiliar with and/or couldn't find the answer in the Cisco documentation. There were also times when I found the exact answer in the Cisco Documentation. However, that was rare.

CHAPTER 27: WHAT TO DO IN THE LAST THREE MONTHS, WEEKS & DAYS

Preparing your moves

By this chapter you may have a good idea of how you might want to go about your studying for the CCIE Lab. This information is sprinkled in the previous chapters; however we wanted to consolidate all of that in one place.

There are five different study schedules that we have suggested in Chapter 37 for your reference. Although each of these schedules suits a different pace there are certain things you need to do to ensure your success.

The **last three months** of preparation should be preferably spent on doing complete eight-hour labs. Initially, completing them in parts and slowly ramping up. In the end many of these should be done in one eight hour sitting to build your focus and stamina. You will be using some time to lookup references for lab tasks that you might have missed in your study. At this point, you may come up with multiple ways to accomplish a certain task. If there is any technology that you are not 100% sure about, this is the time to understand it. A good way is to see how questions on this technology have been phrased in the past ten to fifteen labs. This will give you a very good idea of the variation in questions on that specific technology. Looking back at the short labs is always a good idea.

In the **last three weeks** you should just do complete labs to increase your speed and focus. By this time, you should already have this and all you are doing is polishing and maintaining it. You should think of these as your final dress rehearsals (see Chapter 25 "Jumping into the pool").

One week before the Lab exam you should be doing one last revision. You will have plenty of time to revise, since you have already read all of the topics. Plan it and give yourself two to three days to revise systematically. Divide your study into two or three parts, and go over all of the technologies in detail. Since you have already read and configured these technologies you will be doing a speed read and your full day of revision may finish in four hours. Please go back to read and revise slowly, paying attention details. It is preferred that you do not learn a new technology at this time.

Do not listen to the awful sob stories of others who might be saying things like "the lab was very difficult", "it was impossible to finish", I read everything and there are still topics I had no idea about etc. These will distract you and will add a fear of the unknown. **Have faith and confidence in your study plan.**

The day before the exam should be spent just trying to relax (See

Chapter 29 "The Spacewalk"). Your mind has so much information and will be racing at top speed all of the time. When I $^{(Vivek)}$ went for my Lab the first time I personally gave myself a few topics to read. I was not able to sleep fully and was awake before my alarm went off. I made sure to correct this the next time.

CHAPTER 28: RAPID FIRE

Schedule your lab close to your partners

You and your partner should schedule your actual lab dates close to each other, at the same location. A lab date that is close to your partner will work best for both of you as you will be able to support one another. By that we do not mean that you talk about your actual lab questions.

In our experience, we have seen that once you book the CCIE lab date, you start working harder and with more intensity. Both of **you need to be on the same intensity level** for a successful partnership. Partner B who is taking the lab later can now play a supportive role to partner A to ensure their success. Once partner A is back from his lab attempt the roles reverse which works out well.

In the event that you did not pass, you need to ramp up on your weak areas and ask your partner for assistance. This process would help both of you, because there may be certain points that you missed or misunderstood from the technology standpoint or as to how the questions are worded.

After the first lab attempt, you both know that it is doable and that you have been through the first bump. Now is the time to **sustain the momentum in your preparation and energy level** that is close to that of your partner and vice-versa. This makes moving forward very smooth.

What We Did (by Vivek)

We took turns for our actual lab exam. We also attempted one of the labs on the same day. For our Routing and Switching CCIE, Vivek attempted the lab first, whereas Dean went first for the Service Provider CCIE.

I [Vivek] clearly remember that when Dean passed his second CCIE before me, he came over to my house to support me in my final preparations. As usual, we discussed many topics, but he was very careful and spoke in a very precise way. I understood and respected that as we both signed the non-disclosure agreement.

**** CAUTION ****
Do not tell anyone any details of the actual labs that you attempted. Revealing any lab information to anyone is against Cisco policy and the agreement that you signed and accepted. This will lead to cancellation and/or revoke of your CCIE certification, if you already have one. Candidates may be barred from taking the actual lab exam in the future if they are found in violation of the Non-Disclosure-Agreement (NDA). You can find the latest details about this policy by contacting Cisco or by visiting their website.

**** CAUTION ****

CHAPTER 29: THE SPACEWALK

Lab Test Day

On the day of your exam arrive at the testing center at least ten to fifteen minutes early. Give yourself enough time to take care of any traffic or unexpected delays that you may encounter. If you feel like it, make small talk with the candidates that are also there for their lab attempt. Remember everyone is nervous and anxious. **<u>Listen to the Lab Proctor very carefully</u>**. He will be providing you logistical information about their policies, facility and, most importantly, assign you a rack number. The rack number has to be used across the entire actual lab exam. Their instructions for the lab exam are very crucial and should be followed precisely. Any logistical questions you have should be directed towards the proctor. We want to emphasize, now more than ever, **<u>you need to be calm, cool, collected and in-control</u>**. Although you are in a tense environment, remember all of the effort you have put in the last few months is for this moment. This is the spacewalk you have practiced for.

Once your lab starts, keep track of time in whatever way you feel is best. Don't let other attendees distract you, as you are all in the same boat (tense, and nervous). At the beginning some may be typing fast and others may be talking to themselves. The proctors may be doing their daily work like creating and verifying new labs. At times they may start to bring devices up (for their labs) which may be distracting. You need to focus on your task and disregard your entire surrounding's. Read your lab completely from start to finish. Don't try to answer it, just read it. The objective is to combine activities that will save you time. For example, if you have to enable a routing protocol in one task of the lab and change protocol parameters in another part, and then authenticate it in another part, it is a good idea to complete these tasks in one go. Again, this is not a rule, but just guidance. Some engineers feel that authentication should be done in the end only.

Draw a diagram of your network with at least the interface numbers and IP addresses. This should not take more than two to three minutes. This small investment in time will be very helpful, as you will become very familiar with the network that you will be working with for the next few hours. Keep in mind that these pages will be taken away by the proctor once you have completed your exam.

Use different colors for different protocols and boundaries on the newly made diagram. This will help you clearly see the bigger picture, which is needed to have a smooth redistribution between protocols. You may need to draw more than one diagram. It all depends on what makes you feel comfortable.

It is a good idea to verify each and every task and tally up the points you have completed as you move along. Once the core of the network is done, validate your core network. You may want to consider a ping sweep across the whole network.   You want to make sure that you still have full reachability after every major task you finish.

As you reach lunch time, **save all your configurations and reload all of the routers**. This is a good practice as you will have cleared up any residual configurations that may be affecting you and, also, to verify that everything that you have configured survives a reload.

Depending on which CCIE track you are following, you may have different sections, such as troubleshooting and actual lab. Ideally, you should be finished with enough time to spare for a thorough check of your lab. Pace yourself accordingly.   Do not make any changes in the last 30 to 60 minutes without thinking it through. **Sudden changes might break the lab.** This is also the time to remove all of the aliases and scripts that you may have used to assist yourself during the lab.

What We Did (by Dean)

- Made multiple diagrams

- Used multiple color pencils

- Kept alias file in a notepad so that we could use the no command to remove it.

- Some people keep all of the basic configurations for all routers.

- We reloaded our lab gears at least twice during our actual exam (at lunch and at the end) and we made sure we saved our configurations prior to every reload.

- Keep a list of your ping scripts in a notepad and run it after completion of the task.

CHAPTER 30: THE HOUR AFTER LANDING

You just came out of the exam; after eight long hours, you now have seen the actual lab exam and you assess yourself. Regardless of how you think you did, or how you feel about the exam, you should set your emotions aside and reflect on your experience. You may want to sit somewhere quiet and take some mental notes about what you did and what you can improve upon. This is crucial to your success. These mental notes will come handy as you contemplate and reflect back. **We strongly advise not to turn your cell phone on, at this time.** Make your notes mentally and/or on paper before you begin talking to your family and friends.

Since both of us have so much going on in our minds and we can be forgetful, **we always have a pen and paper handy.** We write down anything that comes to our minds at all times; this helps keep us on track and may work for you as well.

**** CAUTION ****

Do not tell anyone any details of the actual labs that you attempted. Revealing any lab information to anyone is against Cisco policy and the agreement that you signed and accepted. This will lead to cancellation and/or revoke of your CCIE certification, if you already have one. Candidates may be barred from taking the actual lab exam in the future if they are found in violation of the Non-Disclosure-Agreement (NDA). You can find the latest details about this policy by contacting Cisco or by visiting their website.

**** **CAUTION** ****

At times, the solution to a problem may present itself in the most unusual way. When we interviewed CCIEs for this book, one engineer told me [Dean] that two months after his actual lab exam the answer to a problem came to him at the dinner table with his family. This experience never leaves you, nor will the mental notes that you have taken.

Tally up your points and see if you have passed the Lab. Many candidates have the impression that they have already passed the test and would start celebrating. They are the ones who are the most surprised to see that they have failed the exam. Just because you have finished the exam does not mean you followed their guidelines or fully closed any loopholes. The candidate may have configured the lab, but may not have realized that the question had asked him to do it differently.

What We Did (by Dean)

After taking the actual exam, it is imperative to reflect and evaluate yourself without any distractions. So, I spent about an hour in the exam parking lot and took some mental notes. I also wrote down anything that came to my mind including my plans on what to do differently the next time, in case of failure. I found that the mental notes and my action plan would come in handy, especially, once you get the official results. The action plan included immediate registration for next month's lab (in case of a failure), as well as the particular practice labs that I should be focusing on.

CHAPTER 31: THE SECOND ATTEMPT IS USUAL

Majority of CCIE's have failed more than once

Ask any CCIE how many times it took them to pass the lab and you may see some hesitation. Ask them if it took more than one attempt to pass and you will get an affirmative yes most of the time. The majority of those CCIE's took multiple attempts to pass the lab. I [(Dean)] already told you in Chapter 4 that it was difficult, but not impossible. The first attempt gives you the lay of the land and the confidence that you need to do it. It also makes you realize that this is unlike any other test you have taken until now. It is very different and requires you to not only know the technologies, but the ability to apply them as well. The multiple attempts are the battle scars of which you can be proud of. In the end, no one asks you, (except for those seeking CCIE) how many times it took you to be a CCIE? **All that matters is your number and the knowledge you have gained**. Your CCIE will catapult you into a different league and you know you absolutely deserve it.

What We Did *(by Dean)*

Yes, both of us passed the CCIE after multiple attempts. I have seen many colleagues pass on the third and even on the fourth or fifth attempt. We know of a few CCIE's who passed in their first attempt, but those are very few in number. Failure is a part of CCIE and you need to accept this. Keep moving forward till you get your CCIE number.

Share your success stories with us at success@2doubleccies.com

---

A Note From Dean & Vivek:

This guidebook is the sole effort of two fellow engineers like you, who dreamed of spreading what they learned in their quest for the two CCIEs.

If you like our advice and what we have written, then pass on the good word to your colleagues.

Give us a positive review on Amazon, LinkedIn, Facebook and other on-line communities.

Thank you!

CHAPTER 32: SELF ALIGNMENT

If you fail --- shake it off

First and foremost, you should feel proud of where you are and what you have accomplished. Only a few engineers will go this far and attempt to challenge themselves with something like this. If you have taken the exam on a weekday, you will most likely get your results by that evening or the next day. If you took the exam on Friday, you may have to wait until Sunday evening or Monday to find out your results. Once you complete the actual lab attempt, you are likely to have one of these three different reactions:

1) You may feel that you did well and are sure that you passed. (This is a great feeling but the hardest to recover from when you do not pass).

2) You may have mixed feelings and are giving yourself a chance at passing.

3) You know you did not do well and know that you will not pass. If you have passed, then CONGRATULATIONS, YOU DID IT! You can skip the rest of this chapter and go to Chapter 36 "From Ordinary to Extraordinary".

If you have not passed remember that **failure is part of the process. This is the price for success,** which you are willing to pay regardless of the number of attempts.

Passing the CCIE in your first attempt is a possibility. We all want that to happen. However, we have seen that, statistically speaking, it is a small percentage. In our combined experience of thirty plus years in networking and meeting countless engineers, we can count using our fingers how many have passed the CCIE lab on their first attempt. The reality is that, once you get past the lab exam you will most likely never have to go through this again. The exception is if you want to go for a second CCIE or, in the rare case, you don't renew your certification which is every two years.

Do not let this setback overwhelm you; it is natural that you may feel frustrated that you have invested months of your time with no solid results. But, you need to look at your goal of getting your CCIE number. Be in control and continue to execute your strategies. Do not even think about walking away from it. You need to give yourself a 24-hour break and then evaluate yourself objectively. Find the areas for improvement. Your inner mind will tell you the doubts you have, so write all of them down. Once written, you will see that you can easily conquer them in a very short time. If other engineers have achieved this, so can you.

The problem is that we are sometimes our own worst critic. **Do not get discouraged; shake off the negative thoughts** and think of the fame, respect, and monetary rewards that you will have. Your attempt has told you that the lab is not impossible and after this experience you should feel empowered and be ready to use this to your advantage.

If you have talked to other engineers, or even the exam proctors, you will hear all kinds of stories. There are engineers who will read the lab exam and walk away from the lab within a few minutes. Some get so frustrated that they try to sleep in their assigned seat as they do not even know where to start. Now that you have taken the actual lab exam, you will realize why only a few engineers pass. Once you have achieved your certification you will appreciate the high standards of this exam and everything that goes along with it.

To my surprise, when I [(Dean)] was interviewing CCIE candidates who failed, many indicated that answers to some of the questions came to them after days or even weeks of taking the exam. This could happen while working on an unrelated problem or even at a family dinner.

Once you start reviewing your material you may recognize that some of the questions from the actual lab can be found in many of those practice labs. As you have realized by now, the CCIE lab is never about remembering but about understanding and applying technology to solve problems or make the network serve the needs of the lab exam.

The lab does not resemble anything that you may have seen in any production network. Your experiences gained from best practices may hinder you from the assigned task and you may have to think outside the box. For example, you probably won't be running four Interior Gateway Protocols (IGP) on a single router in your enterprise network.

What We Did (by Vivek)

For my second attempt at my Routing and Switching lab (my first CCIE), I thought I had done very well. I was not pressed for time and was able to check my work at the end.

I even reloaded my devices just to make sure. I tallied my score, but there was one small part not working. I did not think that it was that consequential. After coming out of the exam, I was relaxed and absolutely confident that I had passed. I even asked the proctor if he could evaluate my exam faster. When the results came, I was very disappointed. I had failed on this attempt. I knew I was close and the scoring that came back gave me an indication that the one small part that I could not solve contributed towards my failure. I knew that I had to shake it off and move forward. I was close to becoming a CCIE and **immediately registered** for the next available lab date. I promised myself that I would do better and work harder. This is doable!

CHAPTER 33: THE NEXT ROUND

Keep it close

After your CCIE lab results, put things into perspective and try to see what went wrong and give yourself one week per topic in which you think you need to improve or ramp up on.

Always keep your next attempt within no more than four to eight weeks. This is a very important lesson that we learned the hard way. When you come back from your lab attempt, take one or two days off and then get right back to work. Do not break the momentum. Think of your setback as a stepping stone. CCIE Lab is exactly like we described in Chapter 4 "CCIE is difficult but not impossible"; difficult and challenging, but not impossible. All your hard work has brought you this far, so continue to work on technologies that you think you could improve upon and would be to your benefit.

It is important, once again, to emphasize that this book is certification track independent. Each track has its own exam requirements that do change and you need to make sure to understand your track. Confirm with the Cisco website and follow your training program guide that you purchased. We also understand that as of writing this book, the eight-hour

CCIE Lab format is different for R&S as compared to Voice or Security. Nonetheless, the strategies in this book are track independent and still applicable. You can easily adjust these according to your specific needs.

If you ran out of time in your lab exam, set a goal of finishing your practice labs in seven hours. This will give you about an hour to check your results in the real lab. In about two weeks' time you should have a grasp of how much more time is needed to master the technologies you felt you could do better at. **After two weeks, assess yourself and see if you are ready to once again sit for the exam**. Start looking for a suitable lab exam date and reserve the first available slot in four to six weeks (since two weeks have already passed). As soon as you set your next lab date you will go on auto pilot. You will start studying long hours and keep thinking of technologies, labs, and problems you encounter. If you keep on doing this even while sleeping then you are there. Tasks that were difficult the last time will now appear to be easier. Since you have experienced the lab once, you will get your focus and concentration back. Your silly mistakes and errors that caused you grief earlier will be miniscule now. In short, you will be humming along like a well-tuned engine. What used to be a marathon for you will appear like any other race.

What We Did (by Vivek)

I [(Vivek)] made the mistake of giving myself an extended break. When I failed my first CCIE lab attempt, I took about two weeks off and then started to slowly ramp up my study schedule again. At that time, I was not studying with Dean. I procrastinated and soon it had been a month and I realized that I had started to forget things. I couldn't focus for eight hours to do a lab. My typing mistakes went up and I began to drag my feet. That is when Dean came in and he pulled me up. This started our partnership. Encouraged by Dean, I set up a lab date. Had I waited a little longer, or had Dean not encouraged me, I would not be writing this book. I would be buying it.

CHAPTER 34: DO'S

This chapter encompasses all those little things that may seem insignificant but are extremely beneficial.

1. Learn to move between different types of Cisco IOS. Depending on which CCIE you are attempting, you may have to move between devices that have IOS, IOS XE, IOS XR, NX-OS, etc.

   a. So, for example, the configuration of Route Distinguisher (RD) in IOS is different from that in IOS-XR.

   b. The "wr mem" in some versions of IOS-XR is equivalent to commit (be cautious)

   c. There is no Fast Ethernet or Gigabit Ethernet interface in NX-OS. All are simply Ethernet.

2. Reboot time of different platforms is different. Be aware of that.

3. Use of "?" is your friend and enemy at the same time. If you are using help "?" during the core portion of the lab, it usually means that you need more practice. Candidates usually try typing the minimum. For example "wr" for saving configurations and "swi po ac" (switch port access). Use of "?" just wastes time.

4. Use of help "?" towards the end is recommended as you try to go

into different levels in a particular command group and try to find the options available.

5. Use of alias command. Many engineers who are like us, and make a lot of typing mistakes and want to save time make a reasonable list of aliases to use in the lab. We are bad at typing, so we had the following aliases for my Routing and Switching Lab.

   a. s = show ip interface brief

   b. c = config t

   c. sir = show ip route

   d. sion = show ip ospf neighbor

   e. sioi = show ip ospf interface

   f. sien = show ip eigrp neighbor

   g. sib = show ip bgp

   h. sibs = show ip bgp summary

   i. sri = show run | include

       • eg. sri network will display all of the network statements

   j. srb = sh run | begin

       • eg. srb bgp will display configuration bgp onwards.

6. Make sure that, at the completion of your lab, you remove all of the alias commands. I [Vivek] used to type all of my alias commands in a

notepad and have the remove-option also ready with a "no" command in front of all.

7. Another thing that will help you is to go through the initial configurations of your devices. This will help you spot errors and give you a general idea of how things are configured at the start of the lab. I know of a few engineers who recommend saving the initial configurations to a file before you start. Dean did that but I did not.

8. Nowadays, everyone uses DYNAMIPS or GNS3 for lab simulation because of its convenience. It is good for training but do practice on real devices also. Working on a real device is a different feeling. For example, you may notice the difference in time when you do a "wr mem" or the reload times. Many hardware specific features can only be tested on real devices.

9. Make sure to visit your Lab book provider's forums and support group. Many questions are answered just by reading what others have posted.

10. If you prefer to join mailer lists or other CCIE study sites, please join, but make sure you don't get mired by the many what if scenarios people post. Sometimes a simple technology, such as duplex

mismatch, can drag on and many questions can be raised. Each person has his own style of learning and I am not saying what others are posting is wrong. Some conversations are informative and could help with your exam. But if you have a limited amount of time then knowing the ins and outs of how automatic speed and duplex is negotiated deep down to the voltages, is not recommended.

11. Use the same terminal emulator (HYPERTERM, PUTTY, SECURECRT etc), that is being used in the Lab where you are planning to take the Lab exam.

The non-technical do's.

1. If you are sensitive to room temperature, then take a jacket with you. You will be sitting for eight hours and you might start feeling cold.

2. Get used to sitting for eight hours.

3. Check what time the lab starts. I say this because you can choose the venue of your choice depending on whether you are an early morning or a late morning person.

4. Decide when you are going to study for a particular CCIE track, and announce it. I have seen engineers hide this fact. Don't do that. As

soon as you announce this to the world your mind will be committed and start working towards making this happen. For us, friends and family were ready to help. We got a lot of support in many forms, technical help on specific topics, and good tips like the ones we have in this book.

5. Stretch your limits get uncomfortable and step out of your comfort zone. Only then new doors will open and opportunities will come.

6. Troubleshooting is both a science and an art. The science part is the logic used for honing in to the trouble area and the art part is to reach the most probable cause without going through all of the iterations.

7. Make sure you are studying in a very comfortable environment. By environment I mean good lighting, comfortable temperature, ergonomic furniture and other things like coffee, tea, paper, printer, pens, whiteboard, etc.

CHAPTER 35: DON'TS

This chapter encompasses all of those little things that may inhibit your progress.

1. We may be used to multiple monitors on our computer, but it may not be the same in the lab. You need to verify the terminal hardware of the lab by accessing Cisco's website or asking them since things change rapidly.

2. The same holds true for keyboards. Use a standard generic keyboard. I [(Vivek)] had this problem when I went for my first lab. I was using a Logitech fancy curved keyboard. In my lab I had a generic standard keyboard and that slowed me down considerably as I was used to the ctrl + shift+6 keys on my special keyboard.

3. Don't always use RACK1 on your personal labs. Keep changing it to RACK7 or any other number, because you don't know what rack number you are going to get in the actual lab. This will get you accustomed to typing RACK number 5 or 8, which is in the middle of the keyboard and slightly difficult to type as compared to RACK 1. Double digit rack numbers are also not that easy, so try using RACK15 or RACK18.

4. Decide if you will be using tabs or multiple windows for your sessions. For my Routing and Switching Lab I used two windows. One for the routers and another for the switches. I used the "ctrl+shift+6 x" technique to switch between different devices within that window. For my Service Provider lab I had all devices open in different individual windows. None of these approaches are right or wrong, it is your individual preference.

5. Please check to see if the terminal emulator in the actual lab allows use of tabbed session windows. Also validate which emulator is being used, for example PUTTY or SECURECRT or something else. You should get familiar with their features (just in case of any future changes). For example, the clipboard may contain information that you highlight from another window and by right clicking you are pasting that content in your router and therefore, making changes unintentionally. You just don't have the luxury of time.

6. As we have told you throughout this book, do not discuss any details of your lab with anyone. Neither in person, online, or with your instructor. If you divulge any of this you are putting yourself and the other person at risk. Check the Cisco website for detailed policies regarding NDA.

7. Don't go and just attend a boot camp and then attempt the lab. In our experience it has worked for very few individuals. A friend of mine tried that approach and after the boot camp he realized how much he didn't know and needed to study. If you are prepared, then take the boot camp at the end of your studies just a few weeks before your scheduled lab date. The boot-camps may not be teaching new concepts; most of the time and you will find yourself only doing hands on activities.

8. As we mentioned in Chapter 34 "Do's", it is a good idea to join CCIE study groups, but if there are a lot of gloom and doom type of personalities in a particular group; avoid them. You don't need their negative energy; this will only slow you down. If you join a crowded study group, you may not get your questions answered. Some groups are great for networking and relationship building. If you are looking for a good study partner, you may look at these study groups as a vehicle to find your study partner. Therefore, use them as a guiding tool.

9. In our experience, two or a maximum of three is a good number of partners. Having a group of five or more does not really work out. There are always exceptions and our advice is based on our

experiences only.

10. Brute force method. What we mean by this is that you go and take the lab five or six times and remember all of the questions. By the seventh or eighth lab you will be able to pass. BRUTE FORCE DOES NOT WORK. There are no shortcuts to a CCIE and that is the reason there are only a few of them in the world.

CHAPTER 36: FROM ORDINARY TO EXTRAORDINARY

CCIE Success

When I ^(Dean) got my CCIE, I called up my manager to tell him; he was so excited, but I didn't know why. He told me that at the same time that I received my notification for passing the exam, he also got an e-mail informing him of the news (this happened because we were both with Cisco). It stated that he should be proud to have an individual with such skills on his staff and that this certification was a difficult and arduous process and that both of us should be congratulated for such an accomplishment.

From then on, anywhere I went, once they realized that I am a CCIE, they would ask me all kinds of related and unrelated questions or issues concerning their network. At one particular company, the management gave me full access to their network to resolve one of their on-going issues, even though I was there to meet a friend for a social event. Keep in mind that full access comes with full responsibility, so the perception of you knowing all and be asked to troubleshoot will present itself at times. I was not used to hearing, this especially from customers, vendors and even at times, management. This is a great feeling, but don't fall into the trap that you know everything.

What CCIE means is that you can find the answers. The last thing that you want to do is to bring a bad reputation to yourself and lose face with customers.

Since you have accomplished your goal, you should reward yourself. The watch, the motorcycle or that family cruise that you visualized for yourself at the beginning of this journey is now a possibility.

You will find that you have so much time, especially in the evenings or weekends, that you can catch-up with friends and family activities.

Many companies such as including Cisco partners facilitate and encourage your pursuit of CCIE. They may also allocate cash and other rewards for engineers who succeed in passing the CCIE Lab. This means some or all of the costs that you incurred for this exam may be covered by your employer.

Some employers add your CCIE qualification in the company directory and the CCIE logo may be used in your business card. Please follow Cisco's logo usage guidelines prior to printing your new business card. Dean found that during his many years of teaching, one thing that CCIE gave him was instant credibility since many engineers understand what it took to reach this level of expertise.

If you are looking for financial compensation or are thinking of taking on new challenges, this is the time to polish your résumé, market yourself and look for opportunities that would keep your skills sharpened. If you don't use it, you will lose it, so keep up with the technology and build a personal network that can help you with your endeavors. Use this new found fame and success to enhance your career and explore the many opportunities that await you.

Keep in mind that just because you are a CCIE, it doesn't mean that you should sit back and do nothing. Continuous learning is part of the process, so **seek out new ways to learn and grow; don't stay stagnant.** Within the span of two short years you have to recertify your CCIE, by taking the written test either for the same track or on a different track. In the ever changing field of technology, your knowledge is as good as two years; you are expected to keep current and relevant.

What We Did (by Dean)

After reflecting on my accomplishment of passing CCIE exam, and what it took to get there, I realized that my second job was over and I could return to my "normal life." I suddenly had three to four hours each evening and the whole weekend free. Since I was used to taking advantage of every possible minute for my CCIE exam, I decided to take the kids and the family out and spend every minute of that weekend with them. I bought myself the gift that I wanted as my own personal reward and bought the rest of the family their CCIE gift.

When I am teaching, as soon as the students find out that I am a double CCIE they will approach me invariably to find out how they could do the same. This was one of the foremost factors that prompted both Vivek and I to write this book and **provide you with our approach and good honest advice**. There are some people that don't want everyone to have what they have. They may not be as marketable or prestigious anymore. They do not want to lose that fame and authority that they attained with a CCIE to someone else. Both Vivek and I feel that CCIE certification is a life changing experience and will make any engineer appreciate the knowledge and hard work that went into it. It makes you a better person and what you benefit from this experience will profit those around you as well. A Wiseman once said, "The betterment of the world can be accomplished through pure and goodly deeds and commendable and seemingly conduct".

Even after earning our CCIEs, we still pursue the latest technologies and try to take on projects that peak our interest.

Remember to use the same dedication and hard work to achieve all of your goals in life. This kind of preparation and dedication will empower you and change your own perspective of yourself and how others view you. You will enjoy the rewards for many years to come.

CHAPTER 37: SUGGESTED TIMELINES FOR CCIE PREPARATION

Make a map of your path to Success

If you are reading this chapter just after reading one or two other chapters in this book you may not understand clearly what we are suggesting to do in different parts of a timeline. It is recommended that you read the book completely so that you may take full advantage of these strategic timelines. **These suggestions are there to give you direction, but the pace has to be adjusted according to your style and situation**. We are always asked about a guideline for the pace of study so we are providing with five different ones.

1. Private (first timers) Timeline   (Page # 144)

2. Sergeants (One lab attempted) Timeline   (Page # 151)

3. Veterans Timeline   (Page # 158)

4. SEAL (subsequent CCIE)Timeline   (Page # 165)

5. Super Hero (subsequent CCIE) Timeline   (Page # 172)

Private (First timers) Timeline

As the name suggests, this timeline is for someone who is attempting to study for CCIE lab for the first time. This gives you sufficient time to prepare and some extra time for getting into hard-study mode. Depending on your study style, this timeline can compensate for about 40 hours to 60 hours of lead time. (Refer to Chapter 8: Managing External Influences)

Day 1 to Day 15 (15 Days)

Prepare for your journey

Use this period to acquire all of the resources that you will need for the next nine to twelve months. Here is a short list. Please add more if you need to.

1. Decide on and obtain the various CCIE reference books you will be using.

2. Select a training provider and purchase the necessary courseware.

3. Determine what types of hardware you need to simulate your lab.

4. If you plan to buy actual lab hardware, make sure it has the required IOS versions and all of the necessary interfaces and cables for simulating your lab network.

5. Find a location to study on weekdays as well as weekends. It could be a room in your house, a friend's or partner's house, in the library

or your office.

6. If possible, consider your environment, temperature, lighting and other factors which may play an important role in your comfort during study periods. If it's too hot, you feel sleepy. If it's too cold you feel uncomfortable.

7. Select ergonomically correct settings, ie. chair, desk, mouse, etc.

8. Ensure your environment is well lit with both natural and artificial light so that you will be able to see the sun during the day or open a window if need be.

9. Since you will be spending extended hours working on your lab; your muscles and joints may get stiff, so don't forget to stretch as needed, move around and, if possible, do quick pushups (Please take your physicians advice in case of any physical issues).

10. Have plenty of blank paper and color pencils/pens (at least six colors). You will need to make diagrams of your network and mark them for different protocol boundaries and technologies.

11. Have comfortable clothing and footwear.

12. Make sure to have water and healthy snacks during your practice lab sessions.

13. When you feel a need for an extended break, you can exercise while

watching a quick workout video such as Pilates, Tai-chi, Yoga, etc. This gets you refreshed and keeps your mind and body moving.

Day 16 to Day 30 (15 Days)

Journey Begins

Now that you have all of your external resources in place, you need to tune the one last resource, and that is you. Start reading and if you fall asleep that is okay, this means you need more rest and sleep. Catch up on your sleep and prepare yourself mentally. This would also be a good time to get your family, inner circle, boss and colleagues on board. Every moment you should be thinking about how you could find more time for yourself. Take your lunch to work, detach yourself from TV, video games, Twitter, and YouTube subscriptions, etc. Every day, ask yourself, "what you have done today to make your CCIE number a reality?" Every small step counts.

Day 31 to Day 120 (90 Days)

The CORE

This is the core of your preparation. This time should be used to go over the complete Video on Demand. Do all of the short labs that are focused on a specific technology. By the end of this time you should not only feel confident in all of the technologies, but should also have improved your typing skills. If you are going to use aliases then those should be finalized and remembered. You should also be very familiar with using Cisco documentation webpages by now.

Day 121 to Day 150 (30 Days)

Taking the Leap

During these thirty days you should attempt to finish at least five to six full eight-hour labs. Initially, you will be doing it in parts and that's acceptable at this phase. You will frequently get stuck; try to figure out the answer yourself before looking at the solution. Use Cisco documentation as much as possible and learn how to manually search for commands and references. If you still can't resolve the issue, then look it up on the Internet. All of this will add to your knowledge. If you have already spent twenty to thirty minutes, call up your study partner and see if you can resolve the issues together.

By the end of this phase, you should have a good idea of your progress and schedule your lab date around day 240 (about 90 days ahead).

Day 151 to Day 210 (60 Days)

The great push

This is the time when you start doing complete full eight-hour practice labs. We expect you to complete the labs during this phase. By the end of this period, you should be connecting the dots. You should be able to see how technologies will fall into place and how they can be manipulated to accomplish the requirements in the question. Your comfort level will increase as you have already gone through many of the permutations and combinations of technologies that can be presented. You should practice troubleshooting to resolve either an existing problem or by solving your own mis-configuration. Your typing speed and accuracy will further improve and you should be able to concentrate for four to six hours and work without getting tired or need extensive breaks.

Day 211 to Day 240 (30 Days)

Inside the simulator

This is the time when you start doing the labs as if you were taking the exam, almost the real deal. Schedule some time on the rental equipment if you have been using a simulator. Choose a random lab or let someone else choose it for you and think of the lab as if you are at the CCIE testing center. Time allotment for rental equipment is about 11.5 hours per session. Choose the time that is as close as possible to the actual lab time at the testing venue of your choice. You should time yourself and keep a tally. Take a lunch break after four hours.

By working on real live equipment, you realize slight differences. You will see that "wr mem" takes a little longer and device reloads take even longer. Certain features that are hardware specific like queuing, multicast, and layer two features, can be fully tested and troubleshot (which is not the case in a simulator). By Day 240 you should be finishing the labs in about six and half to seven hours (assuming that this is an eight-hour lab). This should give you enough time to verify everything thoroughly and reload the routers just to make sure. We are stressing on this because you will be under slightly more pressure during the real lab test. One small mistake and you can panic and create even more mistakes.

You want to make all of those small mistakes and panic and get over this tendency now.

Day 241 to 270 (30 Days)

Battle stations

Your first scheduled lab attempt should be in this phase. If you pass on your first attempt, congratulations! You did great and should now be thinking of your second CCIE. If you don't pass it is OK. As we said in Chapter 31 "The second attempt is usual". This is normal, so charge ahead un-perturbed. You should start right back up after seeing your score and dig deeper in whatever you think you can improve on. Give yourself a break of no more that 24 to 48 hours, and start again. Depending on how you feel about your preparedness, schedule your second lab attempt as soon as possible (See Chapter 33 "The Next round").

Day 271 to Day 360 (90 Days)

Revisiting the Enemy to conquer

These 60 days combined with the 30 days from the prior phase are reserved for you to schedule and take your next two attempts. Remember, you have to be persistent (keep studying and improving without taking a very long break) and keep persevering.

Sergeant's (One Lab Attempted) Timeline

We call this a Sergeant's timeline, as this is for someone who has some CCIE lab experience. Maybe you are someone who was an unsuccessful in your lab attempt a year ago and gave up after that. This timeline can afford about 30 to 45 hours of lead time (Refer to Chapter 8: Managing External Influences) and has a healthy pace that keeps you on the edge during the entire 10 months.

Day 1 to day 4 (4 Days)

Prepare for your journey

Use this period to acquire all of the resources needed for the next 10 months. Here is a short list. Please add more if need be.

1. Decide on and acquire which CCIE reference books you will be using.

2. Select a training provider and purchase the necessary courseware.

3. Determine what types of hardware you need to simulate your lab.

4. If you plan to buy actual lab hardware, make sure it has the required IOS versions and all of the necessary interfaces for simulating your lab network.

5. Find a location to study on weekdays as well as weekends. It could be a room in your house, a friend's or partner's house, in the library

or your office.

6. If possible, consider your environment, temperature, lighting and other factors which may play an important role in your comfort during study periods. If it's too hot you feel sleepy. If it's too cold you feel uncomfortable.

7. Select ergonomically correct settings, ie. chair, desk, mouse, etc.

8. Ensure your environment is well lit with both natural and artificial light so that you will be able to see the sun during the day or open a window if need be.

9. Since you will be spending extended hours working on your lab your muscles and joints may get stiff, so don't forget to stretch as needed, move around and, if possible, do quick pushups (please take your physicians advice in case of any physical issues).

10. Have plenty of blank paper and color pencils/pens (at least six colors). You will need to make diagrams of your network and mark them for different protocol boundaries and technologies.

11. Have comfortable clothing and footwear.

12. Make sure to have water and healthy snacks during your practice lab sessions.

13. When you feel a need for an extended break, you can exercise while

watching a quick workout video such as Pilates, Tai-chi, Yoga, etc. This gets you refreshed and keeps your mind and body moving.

Day 5 to Day 7 (3 Days)

Journey Begins

Now that you have all of your external resources are in place, you need to tune the one last resource and that is you. Start putting in the time to read. It is okay if you find yourself falling asleep at this point. This means that you need more rest. Catch up on your sleep and prepare yourself mentally. This would also be a good time to get your family, inner circle, boss and colleagues on board. You should spend every moment thinking about how you could find more time for yourself. Take your lunch to work, detach yourself from the TV, video games, Twitter feeds and YouTube subscriptions, etc. Every day, ask yourself "what you have done today to make your CCIE number a reality?" Every small step counts.

Day 08 to Day 90 (83 Days)

The CORE

This is the core of your preparation. This time should be spent going over the complete Video on Demand. Do all of the short labs that are focused on a specific technology. By the end of this time you should not only feel more confident in all of the technologies, but should also have improved your typing skills. If you are going to use aliases then those should be finalized and remembered. You should also be very familiar with using Cisco documentation WebPages by now.

Day 91 to Day 120 (30 Days)

Taking the Leap

During these thirty days you should attempt to finish at least five to six full eight-hour labs. Initially, you will be doing it in parts and that's acceptable at this phase. You will frequently get stuck; try to figure out the answer yourself before looking at the solution. Use Cisco documentation as much as possible and learn how to manually search for commands and references. If you still can't resolve the issue, then look it up on the Internet. All of this will add to your knowledge. If you have already spent twenty to thirty minutes, call up your study partner and see if you can resolve the issues together.

By the end of this phase, you should have a good idea of your progress and should schedule your lab date around day 200 (about 80 days ahead).

Day 121 to Day 170 (50·Days)

The great push

This is the time when you start doing complete full eight-hour practice labs. We expect you to complete the labs during this phase. By the end of this period, you should be connecting the dots. You should be able to see how technologies fall into place and how they can be manipulated to accomplish the requirements in the question. Your comfort level will increase as you have already gone through many of the permutations and combinations of technologies that may be presented. You should practice troubleshooting to resolve either an existing problem or by solving your own mis-configuration. Your typing speed and accuracy will further improve and you should be able to concentrate for four to six hours and work without feeling tired or needing extensive breaks.

Day 171 to Day 200 (30 days)

Inside the simulator

This is the time when you start doing the labs as if you were taking the exam, almost the real deal. Schedule some time on the rental equipment if you have been using a simulator. Choose a random lab or let someone else choose it for you and think of the lab as if you are at the CCIE testing center. Time allotment for rental equipment is about 11.5 hours per session. Choose the time that is as close as possible to the actual lab time at the testing venue of your choice. You should time yourself and keep a tally. Take a lunch break after four hours.

By working on real live equipment, you realize slight differences. You will see that "wr mem" takes a little longer and device reloads take even longer. Certain features that are hardware specific like queuing, multicast, and layer two features, can be fully tested and troubleshot (which is not the case in a simulator). By Day 200 you should be finishing the labs in about six and half to seven hours (assuming that this is an eight-hour lab). This should give you enough time to verify everything thoroughly and reload the routers just to make sure. We are stressing on this because you will be under slightly more pressure during the real lab test. One small mistake and you can panic and create even more mistakes.

You want to make all of those small mistakes and panic and get over this tendency now.

Day 201 to 291 (90 Days)

Battle stations

Your first scheduled lab attempt should be in this phase. If you pass on your first attempt, congratulations! You did great and should now be thinking of your second CCIE. If you don't pass it is OK. As we said in Chapter 31 "The second attempt is usual". This is normal, so charge ahead un-perturbed. You should start right back up after seeing your score and dig deeper in whatever you think you have to improve on. Give yourself a break of no more that 24 to 48 hours, and start again. Depending on how you feel about your preparedness, schedule your second lab attempt as soon as possible (See Chapter 33 "The Next round").

<u>Veterans Timeline</u>

This timeline is surely not for someone who has just started studying for his/her CCIE the first time. This timeline would be best for someone who has studied a great deal for his/her CCIE recently and has most likely attempted the lab. You would be someone who has been thinking about CCIE recently and has a clear opinion about which training provider they would use and a good amount of work experience in technologies that will be in the CCIE Lab exam. This timeline can afford about 20 to 30 hours of lead time (refer to Chapter 8: Managing External Influences) and has an aggressive pace that keeps you on the edge.

Day 1 (1 Day)

Prepare for your journey

Use this period to acquire all of the resources that you will need for the next 265 days. Here is a short list. Please add more if need be.

1. Decide on and acquire which CCIE reference books you will be using.

2. Select a training provider and purchase the necessary courseware.

3. Determine what types of hardware you need to simulate your lab.

4. If you plan to buy actual lab hardware, make sure it has the required IOS versions and has all of the necessary interfaces for simulating

your lab network.

5. Find a location to study on weekdays as well as weekends. It could be a room in your house, a friend's or partner's house, in the library or your office.

6. If possible, consider your environment, temperature, lighting and other factors which may play an important role on your comfort during study periods. If it's too hot, you feel sleepy. If it's too cold, you feel uncomfortable.

7. Select ergonomically correct settings, ie. chair, desk, mouse, etc.

8. Ensure your environment is well lit with both natural and artificial light so that you will be able to see the sun during the day or open a window if need be.

9. Since you will be spending extended hours working on your lab, your muscles and joints may get stiff, so don't forget to stretch as needed, move around and, if possible, do quick pushups (please take your physicians advice in case of any physical issues).

10. Have plenty of blank paper and color pencils/pens (at least six colors). You will need to make diagrams of your network and mark them for different protocol boundaries and technologies.

11. Have comfortable clothing and footwear.

12. Make sure to have water and healthy snacks during your practice lab sessions.

13. When you feel a need for an extended break, you can exercise while watching a quick workout video such as Pilates, Tai-chi, Yoga, etc. This gets you refreshed and keeps your mind and body moving.

Day 2 (1 Day)

Journey Begins

Now that you have all of your external resources are in place, you need to tune the one last resource and that is you. Start putting in the time to read. It is okay if you find yourself falling asleep at this point. This means that you need more rest. Catch up on your sleep and prepare yourself mentally. This would also be a good time to get your family, inner circle, boss and colleagues on board. You should spend every moment thinking about how you could find more time for yourself. Take your lunch to work, detach yourself from the TV, video games, Twitter feeds and YouTube subscriptions, etc. Every day, ask yourself "what you have done today to make your CCIE number a reality"? Every small step counts.

Day 03 to Day 80 (78 Days)

The CORE

This is the core of your preparation. This time should be spent going over the complete Video on Demand. Do all of the short labs that are focused on a specific technology. By the end of this time you should not only feel more confident in all of the technologies, but should also have improved your typing skills. If you are going to use aliases then those should be finalized and remembered. You should also be very familiar with using Cisco documentation WebPages by now.

Day 81 to Day 100 (20 Days)

Taking the Leap

During these twenty days you should attempt to finish at least five to six full eight-hour labs. Initially, you will be doing it in parts and that's acceptable at this phase. You will frequently get stuck; try to figure out the answer yourself before looking at the solution. Use Cisco documentation as much as possible and learn how to manually search for commands and references. If you still can't resolve the issue, then look it up on the Internet. All of this will add to your knowledge. If you have already spent twenty to thirty minutes call up your study partner and see if you can resolve the issues together.

By the end of this phase, you should have a good idea of your progress and should schedule your lab date around day 170 (about 70 days ahead).

Day 101 to Day 150 (50 Days)

The great push

This is the time when you start doing complete full eight-hour practice labs. We expect you to complete the labs during this phase. By the end of this period, you should be connecting the dots. You should be able to see how technologies fall into place and how they can be manipulated to accomplish the requirements in the question. Your comfort level will increase as you have already gone through many of the permutations and combinations of technologies that may be presented. You should practice troubleshooting to resolve either an existing problem or by solving your own mis-configuration. Your typing speed and accuracy will further improve and you should be able to concentrate for four to six hours and work without feeling tired or needing extensive breaks.

Day 151 to Day 175 (25 days)

Inside the simulator

This is the time when you start doing the labs as if you were taking the exam, almost the real deal. Schedule some time on the rental equipment if you have been using a simulator. Choose a random lab or let someone else choose it for you and think of the lab as if you are at the CCIE testing center. Time allotment for rental equipment is about 11.5 hours per session. Choose the time that is as close as possible to the actual lab time at the testing venue of your choice. You should time yourself and keep a tally. Take a lunch break after four hours.

By working on real live equipment, you realize slight differences. You will see that "wr mem" takes a little longer and device reloads take even longer. Certain features that are hardware specific like queuing, multicast, and layer two features, can be fully tested and troubleshot (which is not the case in a simulator). By Day 170 you should be finishing the labs in about six and half to seven hours (assuming that this is an eight-hour lab). This should give you enough time to verify everything thoroughly and reload the routers just to make sure. We are stressing on this because you will be under slightly more pressure during the real lab test. One small mistake and you can panic and create even more mistakes.

You want to make all of those small mistakes and panic and get over this tendency now.

Day 176 to 265 (90 Days)

Battle stations

Your first scheduled lab attempt should be in this phase. If you pass on your first attempt, congratulations! You did great and should now be thinking of your second CCIE. If you don't pass it is OK. As we said in Chapter 31 "The second attempt is usual". This is normal, so charge ahead un-perturbed. You should start right back up after seeing your score and dig deeper in whatever you think you have to improve on. Give yourself a break of no more that 24 to 48 hours, and start again. Depending on how you feel about your preparedness, schedule your second lab attempt as soon as possible (See Chapter 33 "The Next round").

SEAL (Subsequent CCIE) Timeline

We call this a SEAL timeline because this is for someone who is as perfect as a NAVY SEAL. You are someone who is already the best. You know the technologies and probably have a CCIE already and are highly motivated. You may have just finished one CCIE in the past one year. This timeline can afford a lead time (refer to Chapter 8: Managing External Influences) of about 20 to 30 hours only.

Prepare for your journey

You don't need this phase as you know all of this. We leave the activities here only as a reference.

1. Decide on and acquire which CCIE reference books you will be using.

2. Select a training provider and purchase the necessary courseware.

3. Determine what types of hardware you need to simulate your lab.

4. If you plan to buy actual lab hardware, make sure it has the required IOS versions and all of the necessary interfaces for simulating your lab network.

5. Find a location to study on weekdays as well as weekends. It could be a room in your house, a friend's or partner's house, in the library or your office.

6. If possible, consider your environment, temperature, lighting and other factors which may play an important role in your comfort during study periods. If it's too hot you feel sleepy. If it's too cold you feel uncomfortable.

7. Select ergonomically correct settings, ie. chair, desk, mouse, etc.

8. Ensure your environment is well lit with both natural and artificial light so that you will be able to see the sun during the day or open a window if need be.

9. Since you will be spending extended hours working on your lab; your muscles and joints may get stiff, so don't forget to stretch as needed, move around and, if possible, do quick pushups (please take your physicians advice in case of any physical issues).

10. Have plenty of blank paper and color pencils/pens (at least six colors). You will need to make diagrams of your network and mark them for different protocol boundaries and technologies.

11. Have comfortable clothing and footwear.

12. Make sure to have water and healthy snacks during your practice lab sessions

13. When you feel a need for an extended break, you can exercise while watching a quick workout video such as Pilates, Tai-chi, Yoga, etc.

This gets you refreshed and keeps your mind and body moving.

Day 1 (1 Day)

Journey Begins

You are already good at what you do and can easily allocate time for study. You can easily detach yourself from activities like watching football games, movies and other usual entertainment activities. You also have the family and colleagues at work on board, so they help in keeping your workload to a minimum.

Day 02 to Day 60 (59 Days)

The CORE

This is the core of your preparation. This phase will reinforce many of the technologies you already know and fill in any gaps that may exist. This phase should be used to go over the complete Video on Demand. Do all of the short labs that are specific technology focused. By the end of this time, you should not only feel confident in all of the technologies, but also have a good speed of typing without making any mistakes. If you are going to use the aliases then those should be finalized and remembered. You should also be very familiar with using Cisco documentation WebPages by now.

Day 61 to Day 90 (30 Days)

Taking the Leap

During these 30 days you should attempt to finish at least ten to twelve full eight-hour labs. Initially, you will be doing it in parts and that's acceptable at this phase. You will frequently get stuck; try to figure out the answer yourself before looking at the solution. Use Cisco documentation as much as possible and learn how to manually search for commands and references. If you still can't resolve the issue, then search the Internet. All of this will add to your knowledge. If you have already spent twenty to thirty minutes call up your study partner and see if you can resolve the issues together.

By the end of this phase, you should have a good idea of your progress and schedule your lab date around day 155 (about 65 days ahead).

Day 91 to Day 130 (40 Days)

The great push

This is the time when you start doing complete labs. We expect you to complete about twenty labs of your choice twice during this time. By the end of this phase, individual technologies will become very clear in your mind as you have already gone through many of the permutations and combinations they can be presented in. You also have a good practice of troubleshooting as you try to solve the issues that are created by you during your work. This time phase also sharpens your typing skills including both speed and accuracy. You should be able to concentrate for six to eight hours and work without feeling tired.

Day 131 to Day 155 (25 days)

Inside the simulator

This is the time when you start doing the labs as if you were taking the exam, almost the real deal. Schedule some time on the rental equipment if you have been using a simulator. Choose a random lab or let someone else choose it for you and think of the lab as if you are at the CCIE testing center. Time allotment for rental equipment is about 11.5 hours per session. Choose the time that is as close as possible to the actual lab time at the testing venue of your choice. You should time yourself and keep a tally. Take a lunch break after four hours.

By working on real live equipment, you realize slight differences. You will see that "wr mem" takes a little longer and device reloads take even longer. Certain features that are hardware specific like queuing, multicast, and layer two features, can be fully tested and troubleshot (which is not the case in a simulator). By Day 150 you should be finishing the labs in about six and half to seven hours (assuming that this is an eight-hour lab). This should give you enough time to verify everything thoroughly and reload the routers just to make sure. We are stressing on this because you will be under slightly more pressure during the real lab test. One small mistake and you can panic and create even more mistakes.

You want to make all of those small mistakes and panic and get over this tendency now.

Day 156 to 245 (90 Days)

Battle stations

Your first scheduled lab attempt should be in this phase. If you pass on your first attempt, congratulations! You did great and should now be thinking of your second CCIE. If you don't pass it is OK. As we said in Chapter 31 "The second attempt is usual". This is normal, so charge ahead un-perturbed. You should start right back up after seeing your score and dig deeper in whatever you think you have to improve on.

Give yourself a break of no more that 24 to 48 hours, and start again. Depending on how you feel about your preparedness, schedule your second lab attempt as soon as possible (See Chapter 33 "The Next round").

Super Hero (Subsequent CCIE) Timeline

We call this a Superhero timeline because this is for someone who is exceptional as a superhero. There are times when a Cisco partner would want to get a CCIE on their staff in a hurry. I have seen this happen before where one of Cisco's biggest partner will give its top three engineers six months' time for them to totally devote to getting a CCIE. This timeline is suited for them. This is also very suitable for an individual who has just finished a CCIE and wants to go for a subsequent CCIE. This is a very short timeline, as expected. We assume that since you have been through this process once before, that you are familiar with fine tuning and preparing yourself to sit for long hours. You should also be comfortable putting aside time every day of the week and be ready to put in the extra forty plus hours. This timeline worked well for us when we started to study for our second CCIE about a year after our first CCIE. Consider choosing another timeline if you cannot devote the needed 40 hour per week. This timeline is very aggressive and assumes that you and your family are already on board, and that your equipment and choice of Lab training provider have already been decided. You need access to a quiet place to study where you will be undisturbed. You should have all of the other requirements that we have suggested in this book in place and are ready to go. This timeline can afford about 10 to 20 hours of lead time.

Prepare for your journey

You don't need this phase as you know all of this. We leave the activities here only as a reference.

1. Decide on and acquire which CCIE reference books you will be using.

2. Select a training provider and purchase the necessary courseware.

3. Determine what types of hardware; you need to simulate your lab.

4. If you plan to buy actual lab hardware, make sure it has the required IOS versions and has all of the necessary interfaces for simulating your lab network.

5. Find a location to study on weekdays as well as weekends. It could be a room in your house, a friend's or partner's house, in the library or your office.

6. If possible, take control of your environment, temperature, lighting and other factors which may play an important role. If it's too hot you feel sleepy. If it's too cold you feel uncomfortable.

7. Select ergonomically correct settings, ie. chair, desk, mouse, etc.

8. Ensure your environment is well lit with both natural and artificial

light so that you will be able to see the sun during the day or open a window if need be.

9. Since you will be spending extended hours working in your lab; your muscles and joints may get stiff, so don't forget at times you may need to stretch, move around and, if possible, do quick pushups. (please take your physicians advice in case of any physical issues)

10. Have plenty of blank paper and color pencils/pens (at least six colors). You will need to make diagrams of your network and mark them for different protocol boundaries and technologies.

11. Have comfortable clothing and footwear.

12. Make sure to have water and healthy snacks during your practice lab sessions.

13. When you feel a need for an extended break, you can exercise while watching a quick workout video such as Pilates, Tai-chi, Yoga, etc. This gets you refreshed and keeps your mind and body moving.

Prep Day (1 day)

Journey Begins

You are already good at what you do and can easily allocate time for study. You can easily detach yourself from activities like watching football games, movies and other usual entertainment activities. You also have your family and colleagues at work on board, so they help you in keeping your workload to a minimum.

Day 1 to Day 60 (60 Days)

The CORE

This is the core of your preparation. This phase will reinforce many of the technologies you already know and fill in any gaps that may exist. This phase should be used to go over the complete Video on Demand. Do all of the short labs that are specific technology focused. By the end of this time, you should not only feel confident in all of the technologies, but also have a good speed of typing without making any mistakes. If you are going to use the aliases then those should be finalized and remembered. You should also be very familiar with using Cisco documentation WebPages by now.

Day 61 to Day 110 (50 Days)

Taking the Leap with the great push

During these fifty days, you should finish all of the four-hour labs, and complete all of the eight-hour labs that are available to you. Try to finish the eight-hour labs in no more than two sittings. As the individual technologies are clear on your mind, you will be breezing through these labs. You may get stuck at one stage or the other, but should be able to come out of it quickly. You should also get yourself a suitable CCIE lab exam date sometimes during this phase. By the end of this phase, you should be well prepared technology wise. All you need to do now is to increase your speed, focus and accuracy.

You should have a good idea of your progress by the end of this phase and schedule your lab date around day 150 (about 50 days ahead).

Day 111 to Day 140 (30 Days)

Inside the simulator

This is the time when you start doing the labs as if you were taking the exam, almost the real deal. Schedule some time on the rental equipment if you have been using a simulator. Choose a random lab or let someone else choose it for you and think of the lab as if you are at the CCIE testing center. Time allotment for rental equipment is about 11.5 hours per session. Choose the time that is as close as possible to the actual lab time at the testing venue of your choice. You should time yourself and keep a tally. Take a lunch break after four hours.

By working on real live equipment, you realize slight differences. You will see that "wr mem" takes a little longer and device reloads take even longer. Certain features that are hardware specific like queuing, multicast, and layer two features, can be fully tested and troubleshot (which is not the case in a simulator). By Day 130 you should be finishing the labs in about six and half to seven hours (assuming that this is an eight-hour lab). This should give you enough time to verify everything thoroughly and reload the routers just to make sure. We are stressing on this because you will be under slightly more pressure during the real lab test. One small mistake and you can panic and create even more mistakes.

You want to make all of those small mistakes and panic and get over this tendency now.

Day 141 to 190 (50 Days)

Battle stations

Your first scheduled lab attempt should be in this phase. If you pass on your first attempt, congratulations! You did great and should now be thinking of your second CCIE. If you don't pass it is OK. As we said in Chapter 31 "The second attempt is usual". This is normal, so charge ahead un-perturbed. You should start right back up after seeing your score and dig deeper in whatever you think you have to improve on. Give yourself a break of no more that 24 to 48 hours, and start again. Depending on how you feel about your preparedness, schedule your second lab attempt as soon as possible (See Chapter 33 "The Next round").

CONCLUSION

You took the initiative to pursue your CCIE certificate. You have probably spent a lot of time researching all aspects of the variables, criteria, pros, cons and many of the other relevant issues that were involved. You are devoted enough to purchase this guide book, which we believe is the first of its kind for CCIE enthusiasts, and have, hopefully, read all of the way to this point.

We hope reading this book is just one of the many small and large, steps you will take in this life changing journey, which for now is the pursuit of your CCIE number. More importantly, we believe that this pursuance of excellence, a strong work ethic, time and stress management, organizational skills, team work, collaborative effort, expanded knowledge, faith (believing in yourself) and many other skills, mentioned in this book, necessary for obtaining your CCIE will be very useful in achieving greater success and in your career growth. You can also improve on health or even spiritual growth, if you so desire, or any other matter or subject in which you aspire to improve in.

It is our hope that we have, through this book, made a difference in your hunger, appetite and determination to go after and obtain your CCIE.

Never listen to those that tell you it is too hard or not worth it. Only you, through hard work, perseverance, dedication, a positive attitude and determination, can feel the real joy in achieving a goal that, at the beginning, seemed out of reach or even told, by some naysayers, to be impossible or not worth the sacrifice of giving up all of those short term, sometimes immediate, satisfactory pleasures for the greater and more gratifying long term results of achieving a covetous goal, which could potentially guide you towards a more fulfilling and happier road in your life journey.

We hope to hear your success stories, which would be the greatest reward for the hard work we put into writing this book.

A Note From Dean & Vivek:

This guidebook is the sole effort of two fellow engineers like you, who dreamed of spreading what they learned in their quest for the two CCIEs.

If you like our advice and what we have written, then pass on the good word to your colleagues.

Give us a positive review on Amazon, LinkedIn, Facebook and other on-line communities.
Thank You

www.2doubleccies.com

✓ Let us know how you feel about this book.
✓ Let us know 2 or more ways we can improve this book.
✓ Checkout our Video's
✓ Share your experiences. (contact@2doubleccies.com)
✓ Look for our Seminars and Webinars.

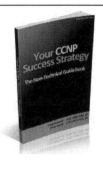

❖ **Your CCIE lab Success Strategy**
  ✓ In French, Spanish and other languages.
❖ **Your CCNA Success Strategy**
  ✓ In French, Spanish and other languages.
❖ **Your CCNP Success Strategy**
  ✓ In French, Spanish and other languages.
❖ **CCNA "Learning by Immersing"** series of eBooks.

Printed in Great Britain
by Amazon.co.uk, Ltd.,
Marston Gate.